IT'S NOT CRICKET

Terry Ravenscroft

Copyright © Terry Ravenscroft, 2013

Cover by Daniel Maney

A RAZZAMATAZZ PUBLICATION

About the author

The day after Terry Ravenscroft threw in his mundane factory job to become a television comedy scriptwriter he was involved in a car accident which left him unable to turn his head. Since then he has never looked back.

Before they took him away he wrote scripts for Les Dawson, The Two Ronnies, Morecambe and Wise, Alas Smith and Jones, Not the Nine O'Clock News, Ken Dodd, Roy Hudd, and several others. He also wrote the award-winning BBC radio series Star Terk Two.

Born in New Mills, Derbyshire, in 1938, he still lives there with his wife Delma and his mistress Divine Bottom (in his dreams).

Also by Terry Ravenscroft

STAIRLIFT TO HEAVEN
STAIRLIFT TO HEAVEN 2 - FURTHER UP THE STAIRLIFT
STAIRLIFT TO HEAVEN 3 - ALMOST THERE
STAIRLIFT TO HEAVEN 4 - STILL HANGING ON
CAPTAIN'S DAY
FOOTBALL CRAZY
I'M IN HEAVEN
THE RING OF THE LORD
SERIAL KILLER
JAMES BLOND - STOCKPORT IS TOO MUCH
INFLATABLE HUGH
DEAR AIR 2000
DEAR COCA-COLA
DEAR PEPSI-COLA
SAWYER THE LAWYER
LES DAWSON'S CISSIE AND ADA
THE RAZZAMATAZZ FUN EBOOK
ZEPHYR ZODIAC
CALL ME A TAXI
GOOD OLD GEORGE
DEAD MEN DON'T WALK

PROLOGUE

It's Not Cricket
1. It is not the done thing. It is not morally acceptable.
2. A 1937 British comedy film directed by Ralph Ince and starring Claude Hulbert. Also a 1998 book by Simon Rae.

Until 1948 the sleepy village of Medlock was quite happy and minding its own business in the county of Medfordshire. In March of that year the government of the day, in a fit of boundary changing - no doubt with the intention of altering the demographic of the electorate for no more reason than to make it more favourable to itself - separated the county into two halves: one half became the county of East Medfordshire, the other half the county of West Medfordshire. The new boundary had the effect of splitting the village of Medlock into two more or less equal halves, and to account for this - and for purely topographical reasons - the two halves were re-named Upper Medlock and Lower Medlock. The dividing line separating the two new counties was the River Medlock, along with its main tributary Blackbottom Brook.

With a single exception the boundary change made little difference to the residents of the villages; they were still the same people living in the same houses going about the same business in the same way. The exception was the owner of The Olde Mill Cottage, a somewhat isolated property on the border, quite literally, between the new villages of Upper Medlock, East Medfordshire and Lower Medlock, West Medfordshire; quite literally because Blackbottom Brook, approaching the cottage from due north of the property, and at that point still near to its source and no more than a couple of feet wide, disappeared underground twenty yards from the perimeter of the property only to emerge twenty yards due south. In which village, and in which county, was The Olde Mill Cottage? No one could say.

More importantly, no one could agree. The parish councils of the two villages and the county councils of the two counties both wanted it and didn't want it; the financial departments of the councils wanted it for the not inconsiderable rates they would exact from the large rambling property set on its half acre of land, whereas the highways departments didn't want it as it would entail their having to keep in good repair the tarmacadam road that passed its front gate. Likewise the respective Gas, Electric and Water Boards wanted it for the revenues it earned them from the supply of their utilities, but as the property was isolated they could see where it might easily cost them more in maintaining those supplies than these monies would amount to.

It was eventually decided, after almost two years of umm-ing and ah-ing, a procrastinating tactic at which local government is especially suited for and adept at, that the four councils would share equally the responsibilities for The Olde Mill Cottage and the income derived from it. It was further agreed, after more umm-ing and ah-ing a, delaying tactic at which suppliers of utilities are just as proficient as is local government - some would even say, with the benefit of the experience of having been on the telephone to their plethora of recorded voices for hours on end, it is the *only* thing they are proficient at - that the Eastern Electricity Board would in future be responsible for all matters electric, the Western Water Board for all matters water, and that the Eastern Gas Board and the Western Gas Board would share equally the responsibilities of supplying gas and receiving the income accruing thereof.

In the meantime the telecommunications arm of the GPO, as it styled itself at the time, which didn't really care from which address it obtained its money as long as it obtained it, continued to send its telephone bills to The Olde Mill Cottage, Medlock, Medfordshire. In the event it didn't receive a penny as the postal arm of the GPO returned their letters to them on the grounds that they were wrongly addressed. Once the GPO had realised it was cutting its own throat - but only after two years of argument and counter argument and more umm-ing and ah-ing between the telecommunications and postal departments - it was agreed that letters for The Olde Mill Cottage addressed to both Upper Medlock *and* Lower Medlock would be delivered. This also benefited the Gas, Electricity and Water Boards as during this period all their bills had also been returned to them.

All of this was of no concern to the owner of The Olde Mill Cottage at the time, Major Roebuck, a retired army officer, who didn't care a hoot to whom he paid his dues, and was more than happy to continue not paying them at all. As it happened it made little difference as he died shortly after his mail delivery had been sorted out, from injuries sustained by an explosion, due to a gas leak, for which neither the Eastern Gas Board nor the Western Gas Board would accept responsibility. (The Eastern Gas Board, noting that there was a violent storm that night, claimed that the explosion had been caused by lightning; the Western Gas Board, possibly having a more imaginative PR department, claimed that the Major, an ex-Royal Artillery munitions officer and a known eccentric, had blown himself up whilst constructing a home-made bomb.)

Before the boundary change anyone anxious for a game of cricket turned out for Medlock in the Medfordshire Conference. At the time Medlock was a thriving club, a club that since becoming a founder member of the league in 1902 had won the league championship on no less than twelve occasions and The Doug Pettett & Dr Leslie Millward League Cup on ten.

For the first two years the new villages of Upper and Lower Medlock continued to play under the banner of Medlock, a happy and convenient arrangement that might have remained to this day had not, in the period between the end of 1950 season and the beginning of the 1951 season, three new teams begged permission to join the league. As the Medfordshire Cricket Conference already had what the league's governing body considered to be too many teams, a situation that meant they had to either begin the season too early or end it too late, bringing with it the problem of possibly running out of daylight before matches were completed, it was decided that to accommodate the new teams, and at the same time solve the running out of daylight problem forever, that the Medfordshire Cricket Conference would be wound up and replaced with two new leagues, the East Medfordshire Conference and the West Medfordshire Conference. As the Medlock cricket ground was in the village of Lower Medlock this placed the club in the West Medfordshire Conference, and it was at this point that it took the opportunity to change its name from Medlock to Lower Medlock. Players who lived in Upper Medlock still continued to play for the team and this remained the case until 1953 when, because the club had a surfeit of players at that time, quite a few of whom rarely got a game, they decided to form a club of their own. A suitable piece of land was purchased at an excellent price from a local farmer - by good fortune the father one of the cricketers who couldn't get a game with Lower Medlock - and after much hard work over the close season a cricket ground for the new team of Upper Medlock was created in time for the start of the 1954 season.

And so the two clubs carried on, each playing happily in their respective leagues, until one Friday night in June of 1957 the decision was taken, in the lounge bar of *The Dun Cow*, Lower Medlock, following a session of alcohol-inspired bragging about the respective merits of the two teams, that they would meet in a 'friendly' at the end of the season. "Then we will see who the better team is," said Harold Edmondson, the Upper Medlock captain at the time, meaning his team. "We most certainly will," replied Lawrence Hornby, the Lower Medlock skipper, meaning his.

It was hoped that perhaps the meeting between the teams would become an annual fixture on the clubs' respective cricket calendars, in the way that friendly fixtures are apt to do.

The first match, in late August of that year, was won in a closely contested encounter by Upper Medlock. It lived well up to the name of friendly, played in a spirit of great camaraderie, with much good-natured banter and praise given where praise was due: bowlers applauded batsmen who had taken fours or sixes off their bowling with fine shots, batsmen applauded bowlers whose deliveries had deceived them and taken their wickets, fielders were applauded for bringing off catches and examples of good fielding. It was all very pleasant.

But not for long.

CHAPTER ONE

Long Leg
1. A fielding position on the leg side near the boundary, almost directly behind the batsman's wicket.
2. What Nicole Kidman has two of.

It had always been Jonny Pickering's plan when he retired from cricket to live out his days in the English countryside; the mild stroke he suffered early in 2013 simply hastened his intentions.

Any non-follower of the game of cricket who crossed the path of the mild-mannered, self-effacing, utterly gentlemanly Jonathan James Pickering would never have guessed in a million years that he was Jonny Pickering, the all-action, courageous, gung-ho England cricket captain, a player whose feats with bat and ball on test match grounds from the Kennington Oval in England to the Adelaide Oval in Australia had caused one of BBC Radio's Test Match Special team to remark that to see him in full flow was 'Like watching Ian Botham on drugs'. (A phrase, incidentally, for which the commentator was hauled over the coals by his employers after over two hundred listeners had rung in to complain, under the impression he had been implying that Botham took drugs, and not, as he had meant, that Pickering played cricket like a sort of supercharged Botham.)

It was ever thus. Throughout his long and glorious career Jonny Pickering had always played the game in the exhilarating manner that lovers of the sport like to see it played. The die was cast when he first turned out at senior level for his local club in the Central Lancashire League at the age of just fourteen years and five months. His fellow batsman, the captain of the side, had stepped forward to meet the callow youngster as he made his way to the crease at the fall of the sixth wicket. Putting a friendly arm around the new batsman's slender shoulders he said, "A word to the wise, young Jonathan. This is a very small ground. No more than forty yards from wicket to boundary in every direction. You can't score three here, it isn't possible, it's not big enough; the ball either goes for a four or it's a single, two at the most. Understand?" Young Jonny took in this sage advice with a serious face and with a nod of the head muttered, 'Yes, Mr Oldroyd' continued on his way to the crease, took guard from the umpire and waited for his first ball in grown-up cricket. The bowler, in no way deferring to the tender years of the new batsman - perhaps by tossing him up a friendly delivery to ensure the youngster wouldn't suffer the ignominy of being out first ball - wound himself up and let loose as fast a ball as he'd bowled all afternoon. Although devilishly quick the flight of the ball was without deviation and came through at a nice hittable height. Needing no further invitation young Jonny drove it confidently through the covers, called "Three" and scampered down the wicket like a greyhound coming out of the traps. And, all credit to him, he ran three before the ball was returned to the wicketkeeper's gloves.

Despite going on to score thirty-eight in just thirty balls after this promising start he was dropped for the next game, probably because during the time he had been running three his captain had only run two and a bit, and had been run out. However, having had time to 'learn his lesson and do as you're bloody told', in the words of the captain, he was reinstated two weeks later, scored a half century, including two sixes on one of the biggest grounds in the league, and had never looked back since.

As handsome as he was talented, during the glittering career that followed Jonny Pickering the man received countless requests from companies keen to harness his popularity to promote their products: hair gel, deodorants, cricket equipment, trainers and multifarious items of sports and leisure clothing were just some of the many items of merchandise he was implored to endorse. There were requests to open fetes, cut the ribbon at the openings of new shops and supermarkets, and appeals to make after-dinner speeches at company's annual shindigs. He turned down all of them. As quiet and reserved off the field as he was flamboyant and colourful on it, away from the cricket field, his day's work done, he valued his privacy more than the cash for which all his contemporaries sold their souls in making hay while the sun shined. Jonny Pickering neither wanted nor needed their tainted money; as a long time member of the England Performance Squad he was well paid for his labours and more than happy with his lot. He never, however, turned down requests that involved charities - he had appeared on *Children in Need* and *Comic Relief* on several occasions - or calls to appear in the benefit matches of cricketer colleagues about to retire from the sport.

There were also invitations to take part in the popular television shows *Strictly Come Dancing* and *Dancing on Ice,* both of which he turned down out of hand. Few doubted that had he accepted and applied to them the same enthusiasm and work ethic he brought with him to the cricket field that he would have waltzed away with the former and skated away with the latter. But it was not to be. He was even asked to appear as a contestant on *Britain's Got Talent*, despite that other than his talent for cricket he didn't possess any other known talent. It was suggested by one observer that such was Pickering's popularity that had he appeared on the show and played a funeral fugue, or perhaps something similarly miserable by Coldplay, on the comb and paper, that he would immediately have been declared the winner; but as with all other requests for his services he had graciously declined the invitation.

The media too, television, radio, and the newspapers and magazines, courted him constantly. He turned down all offers, not wishing to add further to the uneducated guesses, exaggerations and downright lies they already churned out.

There was one offer however, from Quigley's Quavers, that he didn't turn down. But only - with perhaps a nod towards his eventual retirement from county cricket - when he had retired from the test arena and was no longer drawing the generous salary commensurate with that job. (It was reputed that so far as sporting endorsement deals go, and some of them go a very long way, that only Gary Lineker's arrangement with Walkers Crisps paid as much as Jonny Pickering's deal with Quigley's Quavers. Furthermore, thanks to Pickering agreeing the contract strictly on his own terms, he was not, unlike the ex-England footballer, forced to behave like a trained monkey when making TV commercials for the product.)

Like many sportsmen of great achievement he had been offered a knighthood. He had no difficulty in turning it down. A colleague had once remarked that nowadays to be made a knight of the realm had become devalued to such an extent as to be worthless, indeed one could even receive the honour, and had, just for riding a bike. However whilst Pickering didn't agree with this sentiment, and thought it a little unkind, neither could he see much value in an honour that can be bought, provided one has enough money to do it.

For the first three years following his retirement from test cricket in 2010, and still playing county cricket for his beloved Lancashire, his life carried on much as before, but thankfully without all the stress of the grinding test match circuit. Then, one dark week in July 2013, completely out of the blue and completely at odds to his less exacting lifestyle, things changed forever.

Three months earlier he had made the decision to stop playing top class cricket at the end of the current season. At the same time he resolved to sever his connection with Quigley's Quavers when his present contract with them ran out in June. He would then retire completely, both from cricket and the glare of public life. This had always been his intention; only the timing of it had yet to be determined. He informed all interested parties as to his intentions and started making plans for a life beyond cricket.

When making them he didn't have a wife to consider; he had never married, had never even considered marriage. Jonny Pickering, although a man who had never gone out of his way to resist the attentions of the ladies - and had had the occasional fling without ever getting too deeply involved - did nothing to encourage them. (He had found that members of the fairer sex, especially in Australia and to a lesser extent New Zealand, didn't need much encouraging.) He was a man who, as a boy, on reaching the age of puberty and the equipment arriving, would far rather have had a new bat or a pair of cricket boots. (He had heard it said of Boy George that the pop singer would just as soon have a cup of tea as sex, and felt much the same way.) As he grew older his interest in the ladies grew without it ever becoming the obsession it is with the majority of young men, and in adulthood, although he was far too gallant a man to voice it, he regarded women in much the same way as he looked upon dogs - that he quite liked them but there was no reason to have one just because you felt the need to stroke one now and then.

His avowed intention to honour only outstanding commitments proved to be easier said than done. This came as no surprise to him since he had always had great difficulty in saying no to even the most frivolous of requests for his services. So although he would have preferred not to put in yet another appearance at a sportsman's dinner in aid of some charity or other, or turn out in yet another colleague's benefit match, he still found himself carrying out these tasks, for despite his retirement from international cricket he remained as popular as ever; all right, he was no longer the England cricket captain, but in every cricket-lover's eyes he would forever be the great Jonny Pickering, the 'Scourge of the Aussies', the 'Lion of Lords', the 'Tiger of Trent Bridge'. (Jonny had performed just as brilliantly at the Oval but none of the newspapers had been able to come up with a suitable animal beginning with the letter 'O' with which to alliterate it - not even the most crass of the red tops chancing bringing down the wrath of the English cricketing public on their rag by perhaps referring to him as the 'Orang-Outang of the Oval'.)

Whether it was these pesky botherations that caused Pickering to have the mild stroke, the doctor couldn't say for sure. What Dr Purseglove did say for sure, after questioning him thoroughly, was that stress would have been a major factor. Stress, the physician averred, was the cause of the vast majority of strokes and heart attacks. A killer. And although Pickering's stroke had been so mild as to hardly be a stroke at all - in cricketing parlance a tickle down to fine leg rather than a full-blooded drive for six over mid-off - he must take it as a warning and in future avoid *all* stressful situations when and wherever possible. This was sacrosanct; his life may depend on it, he must slow right down; take time to smell the flowers. Pickering told the doctor this wouldn't be a problem as it was his intention to retire. The doctor said it was absolutely the best thing he could do, and the sooner the better.

Jonny Pickering had made the first of his fifteen tours abroad in 1995, the last in 2009, and the cricket apart - which he had revelled in - he had enjoyed the last tour no more than he had enjoyed the first, which wasn't very much at all. A home boy at heart, he had never gone more than a couple of days on tour without feeling homesick, without ever feeling that he would far rather be back home in an English winter than abroad in a foreign summer. Even more so when touring the sub-continent - the cricket there was marvellous, the people of India, Pakistan, Bangladesh and Sri Lanka never less than generous in their welcome, but as far as he was concerned they could keep their hot countries and their hot food; Jonny Pickering, as English as fish and chips, would have much preferred his homeland and fish and chips.

Although born and raised in the Withington area of the

city of Manchester Pickering had always been a lover of the countryside. As a boy he had visited it as often as school and his junior cricket commitments would allow, and in adulthood had spent time in it on his travels through the shires of England in pursuit of his cricket career. It was only natural then that the day after his interview with Dr Purseglove it was to the countryside that he turned in his search for a suitable home in which to settle into retirement. Towns and cities had never had any appeal to him, and had even less nowadays, with their culture of binge drinking, drug dealing and people generally behaving themselves no better than they should and usually a lot worse. There was none of this to be had in the countryside, at least none of which he had ever come across, and even if there was he was sure there wouldn't be very much of it.

A week later, after turning down the Lake District as being peaceful but too wet, the Cotswolds as being peaceful but too touristy, and Snowdonia as being peaceful but too Welsh, he plumped for one of the Medfordshire counties, either East or West would do, it didn't make much difference, their wealth of pleasant countryside made them equally desirable.

In fact the Medfordshire counties were little else *but* pleasant countryside; acre upon acre of it with just the occasional village here and there and one town, Middleham, of any size. But everything he needed was to be found there and very little he didn't; a rolling landscape in whose verdant hills and valleys he could take long relaxing walks; two important RSPB bird reserves within ten miles, where he would revive the interest in ornithology he'd had as a boy but had had precious little time to enjoy as a man; fishing, which he had never done but had always had a hankering to try - it was reported that there was excellent salmon fishing to be had in the River Medlock, the picturesque river that wended its way through the two counties. And should he by some strange chance become temporarily bored with rural life, the sea, with its bracing air and beaches and sheltered coves, was just twenty miles away.

After a short search he found the ideal property, The Olde Mill Cottage, an eighteenth century thatch-roofed, mullion-windowed, whitewashed-stone property. It was exactly what he was looking for, and vacant possession to boot. In this country retreat, which even had the archetypal roses growing round the front door, he would settle into his well-earned retirement. He would read a lot, do a spot of gardening when it took his fancy, maybe take up painting, just another of the things he wouldn't mind having a crack at but had never had the time. He hadn't been bad at painting at school, usually landscapes remembered from trips into the nearby Cheshire and Derbyshire countryside; the art teacher had been quite complimentary about his water colour of Castleton's Mam Tor and he still had a study of Kinder Scout from Hayfield village that he'd painted as a fifteen-year-old. He might even write his autobiography; God knows he had been asked often enough by publishers anxious to cash in on his name, but had always managed to ward off. But if he did agree to write his life story it would be on his terms, not theirs. And his terms would be that he would write it as and when he pleased, at his own pace, and not to some pre-ordained deadline; he had read too many autobiographies about the latest sportsman to hit the top, slung together with the help of a ghost writer with the maximum of haste and the minimum of depth.

Yes, life in the country would be just the ticket. In his

chosen heaven on earth he would cocoon himself from life's troubles and enjoy the rest of a stress-free life. He sighed with happiness at the very thought of it; it all sounded too good to be true.

    It was.

CHAPTER TWO

Chinaman
1. *A ball bowled by a left-handed bowler to a right-handed batsman that spins from off to leg.*
2. *A male native or inhabitant of China.*

"You're all right for the twenty-third are you?" said Les Duckworth quite anxiously. Due to the Upper Medlock cricket team's paucity of playing strength there was always a trace of uneasiness in the voice of their captain and opening bat when enquiring about the availability of his team mates for forthcoming fixtures.

"All right for what?" said Wayne Gibbon.

"Bloody hell, Gibbo!" With a despairing look on his weatherbeaten face that said 'You see what I have to put up with' Duckworth turned to his vice-captain Andy Bristow, who along with Franny Francis and Billy Harris were the other two members of the team seated at a corner table in the lounge bar of *The Grim Jogger* enjoying their regular Friday night session. Or at least they were enjoying it up until now - they were all well aware what their skipper was like when he got a bee in his bonnet about something, and any lack of enthusiasm by one of the team was guaranteed to attract a whole swarm of bees to his bonnet.

Duckworth scowled at Gibbon in the hope that this visual comment on what exactly he thought about the all-rounder's reply might have a fortifying effect on him; not that he imagined for one moment that it would, unless Gibbon's IQ had suddenly shot up to a level not previously hinted at. "The match against Lower Medlock, Wayne, the match against Lower Medlock," Duckworth spelled out with all the patience he could muster, which, truth to tell, was never very much.

"Oh that," said Gibbon, as though the local derby were just any old game.

"Yes, *that*," said Duckworth, then, when it became evident that Gibbon wasn't about to enlarge upon his answer, "Well are you available or aren't you?"

Gibbon a tall, loose-limbed man of thirty, the average age of the Upper Medlock team, whose current ages ranged seventeen to forty-seven, a typical spectrum for village cricket teams, thought about it for a moment before answering. "Yes, I should be able to manage it; I don't think I've anything else on that day."

The annual fixture between the two Medlock villages might have been just any old game to Gibbon but it certainly wasn't to Les Duckworth and the rest of the Upper Medlock side (with the exception of star batsman Piggy Higginbottom, who didn't like playing against Lower Medlock as they habitually sledged him without mercy due entirely to a past indiscretion.)

"You're quite sure now are you, Wayne?" said Duckworth, the anxiety still in his voice despite Gibbon's assurance. "I mean we're going to really need you if we're going to bowl out that load of stuck-up, shower of shit,

Lower Medlock snotgobblers."

Duckworth wasn't exaggerating. Over the years Upper Medlock had fielded good sides and bad sides and the current line-up was well to the lower end of the quality range, if not at the very bottom. The only thing that elevated them from mediocre to well below average was a decent bowling attack: a very good fast bowler who got his wickets by the sheer pace and bounce of his deliveries; an almost as good medium-pacer who employed swing and variations in the line and length of his deliveries; and a very steady slow bowler, an off-spinner, who could not only be relied on to chip in with a wicket or three but was also adept at finding a few maiden overs when the opposition's run rate needed slowing down. The trouble was that the fast bowler, the medium-pacer and the slow off-spinner were all Gibbon. Who could only bowl at one end at a time. (Although on one occasion, with a rare victory just about on the cards, Duckworth had tried to bowl Gibbon at both ends at the same time, claiming that the MCC had recently made a change to the rules whereby a bowler was allowed to do this for a maximum of six overs - a blatant lie that had cut no ice whatsoever with the captain of the opposing team and the umpires, who reported him to the league for ungentlemanly conduct, for which he received a rap on the knuckles and a three match suspension.) This meant of course that while Gibbon was either bowling fast, fast medium or slow, at one end, taking a wicket every now and then and finishing up with collective figures of, say, 9 for 84, the four bowlers at the other end, Harris with his off cutters, Eckersley with his donkey drops, Bristow, a left-arm spinner who could bowl the odd Chinaman, and an odd Chinaman, Woo Sang, who bowled whatever came into his head during his run up, were collectively getting figures of, typically, 1 for 150. (The '1' in this statistic had yet to be achieved by Woo Sang, owner of the esteemed *Perfumed Garden Chinese Chippy*, who only made the starting eleven because the team invariably struggled to field a full complement of players; and perhaps more importantly the fact that he gave his team mates free prawn crackers and a twenty per cent discount on takeaways at weekends and Bank Holidays.

"It's not one of your bloody inconvenient *Flog It!* weekends then?" Duckworth went on, still not completely convinced he would have the services of his star bowler for the blood match.

Gibbon, obviously disappointed, shook his head. "Too far, Aberdeen."

Duckworth shot him a warning look. "And we can do without another episode like all that bollocks last year."

"No chance," said Gibbon waving his captain's caution aside. "Once bitten."

Duckworth wished he was as convinced of this as Gibbon appeared to be. Knowing him as well as he did he suspected that there was every chance he would be bitten a second time, if not half a dozen more times. The ideal situation for the Upper Medlock captain would be if Gibbon were to be tethered to the end of a very long, strong rope whilst he went about his cricket. However, sensing that Gibbon would object to this stricture on his freedom, he would have to settle for keeping a very close watch on him, especially during the tea interval.

The object of Duckworth's worries drained the remainder of his Old Stumpy best bitter and eyed the emptiness of the glass for a moment or two before bringing it down with a thump on the table and looking at it pointedly, as though the refilling of it with another pint of the same would help to confirm his availability for the match. Gibbon was a man of few words and, apart from when he was bowling his slow off-spinners, little subtlety.

Duckworth, thanking his lucky stars that Gibbon would at least be available at the start of the match, and hoping that between now and then he could come up with a guaranteed way of keeping him there for the duration of the hostilities, set his worries aside for the time being, at the same time hoping and praying that *Flog It!* valuation days never strayed south of Aberdeen ever again.

It was a long-standing ambition of Upper Medlock's star bowler to appear on the BBC antiques programme on nationwide television and be seen by all his friends and relations. All right, it may not be for the fifteen minutes of fame he would prefer, but five minutes of fame would do very nicely thank you. His aspirations in this regard had already cost the club dearly on six occasions during the current season, three times that number since Gibbon had been seized with the idea four years earlier. Thus far, despite all his efforts, he hadn't even got close to being one of those chosen to appear before the cameras along with the antiques they had brought along to be valued by the *Flog It!* valuation experts. Bristow, rather unkindly, had once told Gibbon that the only thing he was flogging was a dead horse and Gibbon, although hurt, hadn't argued with him as he suspected he might well be right.

The problem was that he didn't possess anything worth valuing, neither something intrinsically valuable nor something desirable for its rarity or curiosity value. Leaving aside the large cast iron Victorian mangle, which he had managed to muscle into the boot of his Fiat Panda without too much difficulty, before finding on arriving at the *Flog It!* venue that very heavy awkward-shaped objects are much more difficult to muscle out of the boot of a Fiat Panda than they are to muscle into it - and which ended up costing him more than he hoped to make for it when he was forced to hire a fork-lift truck to lift it out - the most promising thing he possessed was the World War II German helmet he had acquired from eBay for £80, buyer collects. He had collected, and lugged it, for it too was made of iron, and although not as heavy as the Victorian mangle was by no means light, from venues as far south as Hastings to as far north as Glasgow, as far west as St Ives to as far east as Norwich, without it once impressing any of the on-camera experts, none of whom had given it more than the most cursory of examinations before continuing down the line of people who had hopefully brought along their antiques that day. The half dozen or so off-camera experts who had valued the helmet thus far had priced it at anything from £40 to £90, the majority of them, disappointingly for Gibbon, nearer the lower end of the price range. One of the experts had mentioned that his valuation would have been higher, maybe as much as £100, if the helmet had had a swastika emblazoned on it. Before attending the next valuation day Gibbon painted the infamous symbol of the Nazi Party on the helmet, which may have increased its value, but as yet had failed to increase the interest of any of the on-camera valuers, who continued to pay it scant regard. (One of them, James Lewis, before passing quickly on to something more interesting, said it would have been more valuable, possibly as much as £120, if some bloody idiot hadn't painted a swastika on it.)

When it had become clear that their star bowler's *Flog It!* ambitions were having a depleting effect on the team's performances, and that the German helmet had about as much chance of appearing on television as Ant or Dec have of winning *Brain of Britain*, Duckworth called an emergency meeting of the cricket committee to discuss the matter. After much debate and prevarication - cricket committees being no different than any other committee when trying to come to a decision on anything more tricky than what type of biscuits to have with the coffee - it was decided to purchase for Gibbon, from club funds, an antique that would give him a much better chance of appearing on *Flog It!* than the German helmet. (The offer of a large iron chandelier by one of the committee was turned down on the grounds that Gibbon had already experienced enough trouble with iron *objets d'art* with the Victorian mangle and the German helmet.) Taking the advice of Justin Threlfall, the club's wicketkeeper, himself a keen viewer of *Flog It!*, it was decided by a vote of five to one - the one being the member who had offered the iron chandelier, who was in a bit of a strop about his offer being turned down - that an item of pottery would be the ideal thing to go for, it being advised by Threlfall that pottery was selected for valuation more frequently than other antiques. Clarice Cliff, Royal Worcester, Troika, Ruskin, Charlotte Rhead and Wedgewood, all regularly featured on the show were considered, but in the end, again following Threlfall's advice, a very nice *circa* 1923 Moorcroft vase in one of the rarer patterns was purchased at a cost of £210. Gibbon was also furnished with a nice back story by Jack Robinson, a member of the side with literary pretensions who had once had a short story published in the *War Cry*, that claimed Gibbon had come across the vase at a car boot sale, it had been priced at just £4 and Gibbon, completely unaware of the value of the piece, had knocked the car booter down to

£2.50. Robinson had assured the committee, and Gibbon had concurred, that the *Flog It!* experts were always pleased when this sort of thing happened as it gave them the chance to express wide-eyed amazement that such a thing could still occur in this day and age, and complain that it never happened to them. In addition Robinson concocted a story to the effect that any proceeds from the sale of the vase would be donated by Gibbon to local children's charities (it wouldn't, it would be going straight back into the cricket team's funds without touching the sides, good God man they weren't made of money), which would further enhance Gibbon's chance of being one of those chosen to appear on the show. Robinson further suggested that it would do Gibbon's chances no harm at all if he let it drop that his mother had a terminal disease but Gibbon turned this down as he loved his mother and didn't wish to tempt providence.

At the very next valuation day that Gibbon attended, at Buxton's Pavilion Gardens in the Peak District, the ploy was successful, as far as it went. The problem was that it only went as far as an on-camera expert, having spotting Gibbon seated in the queue cradling the Moorcroft vase, had approached him, whereupon Gibbon, in his excitement at seeing the expert eagerly heading his way, had dropped it. Fortunately the floor was carpeted and the vase didn't break. Unfortunately it broke two seconds later when in the act of picking it up he dropped the German helmet, which he had also brought along as he still had every confidence in it, and it had landed squarely on the vase, smashing it to smithereens.

"Getting them in then or what?" said Gibbon, after neither Duckworth nor the others had shown any signs of recharging his glass. Strictly speaking, for everyone else had already stood their corner, it was Gibbon's turn to put his hand in his pocket; however Gibbon had a habit of trying to duck out of his round if he thought he could get away with it and being reminded of his value to the team had presented him with just such an opportunity.

In the event, it was a fifth member of the Upper Medlock cricket team, Shane Spragg, who bought the next round. But only after he had broken the most wonderful news to his team mates. It was news of such tremendous import that in his eagerness to break it he walked straight past the bar without breaking stride, something he had never been known to do in over two decades of dedicated drinking since first becoming a regular of *The Grim Jogger* at the age of fifteen, and which caused the landlord to almost drop the glass he had been drying.

"What do you think has happened?" Spragg said breathlessly, quite unable to keep the excitement out of his voice even if he had wanted to, which he didn't because he was a man who liked a nice drama. "It's something fucking marvellous."

"*Flog It!* has been axed?" said Duckworth, but more in hope than expectation.

Spragg was grinning like the cat that had not only got the cream but a year's supply of Whiskas with it. "Better than that."

"Go on then."

"You'll never guess who's come to live in Upper Medlock?"

"Who?"

"Guess. But think mega. Think who would be the absolute best person possible in the whole world to come to live in the village."

"*Beyoncé?*" said Francis without hesitation but much

hope.

Spragg shook his head. "Think cricket."

"*Beyoncé* naked apart from a pair of stumper's pads," said Francis, his face lighting up at the prospect.

Duckworth groaned. "Bloody hell, Franny, don't you ever think of anything but sex?"

Francis shrugged. "A man can dream, can't he?"

"Anyway, if *Beyoncé* did come to live here she wouldn't give the likes of you a smell. And even if she did flash her booty in your direction you wouldn't know what do with it," he added cruelly.

"Who is it then?" said Harris, as anxious as the others to know the identity of the mystery person who had moved into the village.

"Did any of you see that documentary about disabled paedophiles on Channel Five last night?" said Bristow.

Francis had and grinned at the recollection. "Hey, that one-legged bloke was a scream, wasn't...."

Duckworth turned on Bristow angrily, cutting Francis off in mid-stream. "*Don't* change the subject!"

"I was only...."

"Never mind what you were only; we are *talking* about who has come to live in Upper Medlock."

"Has a one-legged paedophile come to live in the village?" said Gibbon, who hadn't been paying too much attention, but now, a keen fan of *Embarrassing Bodies* and *The Undateables* as well as *Flog It!,* his interest aroused.

"What?" said Spragg.

Pausing only to throw a filthy look in Gibbon's direction, Duckworth, fast approaching the end of his tether, the club captain not being a man noted for having a long tether, said, "For fuck's sake, Spraggy, just tell us who exactly is coming to live here and get it over with will you!"

"I suppose it'll like give the kids more chance," said Gibbon thoughtfully. "To run away, I mean."

"Run away from who?" said Francis."

"A paedophile. I mean if he only has one leg."

"He could hop fast," suggested Harris. "There was a bloke in the Paralympics who could hop faster than I can run, went like the bloody clappers he did." His brow wrinkled as he tried to recall the incident. "I don't know if he was a paedophile though."

During this exchange Duckworth had taken a long drink of his pint of Old Stumpy. It did nothing to soothe his temper. "Jesus Christ on a bicycle, will you stop going on about paedophiles!" he now said. "And you, Spraggy, tell us who's come to live here or I'll hit you with this pint pot."

"You'll never guess," said Spragg, anxious to hang onto his wonderful news for a moment or two longer.

"I don't *want* to bloody guess," said Duckworth, "I want to bloody know."

"Moved himself into The Olde Mill Cottage just this afternoon, just hours ago."

"*Beyoncé* in...."

"For Christ's sake will you stop going on about *Beyoncé*!" Duckworth raged, his face taking on the murderous look it often did when talking to Francis.

"All right, all right, keep your wig on," said Francis, a bit peeved. He turned to Spragg. "Lady Gaga then?"

"I'll fucking gag you if you don't put a sock in it," said Duckworth, his patience now completely exhausted.

Francis raised his arms as though to ward off a blow. "Sorry, sorry Only joking, skipper."

"Well don't. And you Shane, stop pissing about and tell

us who it is."

Spragg took a step backwards to give himself a little space for the announcement, paused for effect, and proclaimed, rather like a toastmaster proposing a toast to a particularly desirable guest of honour. "*Only* Jonny Pickering."

Duckworth's mouth fell open. His lips trembled in a vain attempt to say something. When after a moment or two he managed to close his mouth enough to form words he said, in absolute awe, "Jonny Pickering?"

Spragg nodded eagerly. "I told you it was mega, didn't I."

"*The* Jonny Pickering?"

"None other."

"Well bugger me."

"Who's Jonny Pickering?" said Francis.

"*Beyoncé*'s husband," said Bristow. "He'll no doubt be bringing *Beyoncé* with him. So I'd lay in a supply of condoms if I were you. I can recommend the ribbed ones with the warthog's head on the end; it's the tusks that make all the difference."

In the unlikelihood that Francis might have fallen for this cruel lie Duckworth put him right. "Jonny Pickering is only the greatest all-rounder ever to play cricket for England."

"Oh," said Francis, his memory possibly having previously been fogged by visions of *Beyoncé* naked in a pair of stumper's pads, "*That* Jonny Pickering."

"*That* Jonny Pickering," said Duckworth. "*Only* the Jonny Pickering who almost single-handedly won back the Ashes after sixteen years. *Only* the Jonny Pickering who took 15 for 110 and scored a century in the first innings and a double century in the second test at Old Trafford." Duckworth sat back in his chair, placed his hands on more than the beginnings of a paunch and gave a huge, contented sigh. "This is it, lads. It's arrived. The Golden Ticket. The winning number of *Euro Millions*. We've already won the match against them Fancy Dan gits from Lower Medlock. Once they find out Jonny Pickering is playing for us I'll be surprised if they even turn up."

"*If* he'll play for us," said Harris, throwing water on the burning fire of Duckworth's prognosis.

"What do you mean if he'll play for us?" scoffed Duckworth. "Of course he'll play for us. Why wouldn't he play for us?"

CHAPTER THREE

Short Leg
1. A fielding position on the leg side near to the wicket.
2. What a dwarf has two of.

"By use of which other cooking implement might a supreme of local chicken be fried, exactly?"

"Sir?" There was more than a trace of weariness in the waiter's voice.

Marchbank, the poser of the question, enlarged on it. "Other than a pan?"

Looking as though she would far rather be somewhere else, preferably a place far away from her husband, Bethany Marchbank elbowed her spouse sharply in the ribs. "Jerrold, behave!"

Marchbank, taking no more notice of his wife than he usually did, carried on regardless. "A bucket, perhaps? Is it possible to have one's supreme of local chicken fried in a bucket? Or a coal scuttle, mayhap?"

The waiter bit his lip. He would far rather have bitten Marchbank's bollocks. It wasn't the first time that Marchbank had had fun at his expense; a couple of Fridays ago he had asked him where, if not from a garden, garden peas came from, a fucking car park? Having to work in Lower Medlock was bad enough; having to wait on the captain of their cricket team didn't bear thinking about. But jobs were hard to come by these days and needs must.

"Well?" said Marchbank, when it became obvious that a reply from the waiter wasn't forthcoming.

"Just a frying pan, sir."

Taking great pleasure in the waiter's discomfort, his enjoyment heightened by the fact that not only was the man a resident of Upper Medlock but, even better, was a member of its cricket team, Marchbank said, "Well in that case - and in the absence of a bucket or a coal scuttle - or, failing those utensils...."

"Oh give over, Marchers, for God's sake," said Percy Penrose, the club's vice-captain, laughing and clutching his stomach in exaggerated enjoyment at his friend's scathing wit. "You'll have us wetting ourselves."

"Yes, give over why don't you?" said Penrose's wife, Penny, but unlike her husband meaning it, bored with Marchbank's loutish behaviour, which was nothing new.

However Marchbank was in full swing by now, in full arsehole mode as his wife would say. "Or, failing those utensils, a number nine shovel perhaps?" he said, with an exaggerated enquiring raise of the eyebrow.

Rodney Roderick, another member of the Lower Medlock cricket team, as amused by his captain's antics as Penrose, leant without ceremony over his wife to slap Marchbank heartily on the back. "You're a caution, Jerry, you really are."

The caution's wife said, "He's a bloody pest." She hissed at her husband through tight lips. "Everyone is looking at you."

"Let them." If Bethany's warning was designed to

encourage her husband to cease his baiting of the waiter it was destined to failure. Marchbank liked people looking at him; he liked being the centre of attention, positively bathed in it.

"So will you be having the chicken, sir?" said the waiter, anxious to move on before Marchbank spotted a new addition to the menu, *Hand-glazed Pacific Ocean black cod fillet'*, and enquired if perhaps sometimes the chef glazed it with his feet. If Marchbank did the waiter had already made up his mind to say balls to the job and punch him full in his self-satisfied fat face.

But instead Marchbank said, with a sigh of despair that would have done credit to Brian Blessed auditioning for *King Lear*, "Well with my taste buds whetted for supreme of local chicken, and in the apparent non-availability of any of the other frying devices I have suggested, I suppose I have no alternative."

The waiter took his reply as a yes and turned his attention to Marchbank's better half. "And for madam?"

The three couples were dining in *The Skillet*, the restaurant wing of their local, *The Dun Cow*, a public house that tried to appear older than it was by the addition of fake oak beams and exposed stone walls, its attempts in this regard somewhat offset by the plastic juke box. The food was very acceptable though, despite everything on the menu being garnished with a generous helping of verbiage. Dining at *The Dun Cow* on Friday evenings was the Marchbank party's way of divesting itself of the worries of the workaday week and relaxing smoothly into the weekend.

As the waiter moved on to Stephanie Roderick, having taken Bethany's order of *Scampi cooked our own very special way with thrice-fried chunky chips and market fresh vegetables of the day*,

Marchbank said, "All looking eagerly forward to the twenty-third, are we?"

His question, although he didn't qualify it as such, was directed solely at the men in the party, as was almost all his conversation in mixed company. He was therefore surprised when Penny Penrose said, "Oh are you going too?"

Marchbank frowned. Going? What was the silly tart talking about? The fixture was at home this season; she ought to know, she and Bethany were in charge of the teas. He regarded her baldly. "What's that?"

"I didn't think a Barry Manilow concert would be your sort of thing?"

"What?"

"The Barry Manilow concert? I didn't think it would be quite your bag?"

Marchbank looked at her even more puzzled. "Barry Manilow concert? What Barry Manilow concert?"

"He's appearing at Middleham Castle on the twenty-third." Penny smiled fondly at the prospect. "Outdoors in the grounds. Perce and I are really looking forward to it."

Almost sure Penny was pulling his leg, but not sure enough for alarm bells not to start sounding in the distance, Marchbank said to Penrose, "I assume your little lady is telling porkies, Penners? I take it she is pulling my leg?"

Penrose squirmed uncomfortably in his seat and suddenly found a previously undisclosed interest in the large stag's head hanging on the opposite wall.

Marchbank's eyes opened wide in disbelief. "She *isn't* having me on?" Penrose remained deaf to his captain's entreaties. "Penners!"

Penrose reluctantly wrenched his gaze away from the stag and nodded dumbly.

Marchbank, the alarm bells now clanging away ten to the dozen, could scarcely credit it. "But....I mean it just can't be....I mean there's the match against Upper Medlock."

Penrose couldn't have looked more sheepish if he'd had the number 27 painted in red on his side and was standing in a field baa-ing between mouthfuls of grass. He managed an apologetic smile and bleated, "Sorry."

"Sorry? What do you mean, sorry? What about...." The rest of the sentence died in Marchbank's mouth as the enormity of the situation hit him again. "Jesus wept! This is a disaster. Why didn't you tell me before for fuck's sake?"

Penny Penrose answered for her husband. "We didn't know ourselves until Wednesday. My sister Polly and her husband were going with friends. However the friends had to cry off and they offered their tickets to us. Of course we leapt at the chance."

Marchbank looked as though he was about to leap on Penrose and commit grievous bodily harm upon him. "And you put going to see some big-nosed curly-headed hairy-arsed American wanker who can't sing for toffee ahead of the Upper Medlock game?"

"I wanted to do something nice for Penny," said Penrose, blushing, but omitting to say that the reason he wanted to do something nice for Penny was that a few days previously she'd caught him in a compromising position with their au pair. Now he looked fondly at his wife and patted her on the knee. "The old girl deserves it, having to put up with me as she does."

Marchbank's first thought was to try to arrange for the assassination of Barry Manilow, an action that in his opinion would not only solve the problem of his player shortage but would do the rest of the world a favour. However he could see that this might be construed as being a bit too extreme, although not by much. He was not, however, a successful solicitor of twenty years standing, many of them spent representing defendants in the minor courts, because he was unskilful in the art of spotting a weakness in the opposition's argument. He went on the attack. "But, I mean, you don't *have* to go, do you? You are not *forced* to go?"

"Yes he is," said Penny firmly. A sharp glance at her husband informed him that his part in the conversation was over, an action completely wasted on him as in the meantime the stag's head had attracted his undivided attention again.

Marchbank could see that nothing short of throwing himself on the mercy of the court would swing the case for the defence. "But we need Percy, Penny," he pleaded. "I implore you. I beg you. There's already every chance of us being a man short as it is."

"Actually there are another two seats for the taking," said Penny, not only remaining completely unmoved by Marchbank's pleadings but showing less mercy than Judge Jeffries. "Because the day after Polly told me her friends couldn't go she rang again to say that she and Mark wouldn't be able to go either...." She looked around the table. "So if any of you would care to join us?"

"No they bloody well would not like to join you!" screamed Marchbank, losing it completely. "For crying out loud, haven't I just said that we're already a player short? It's already going to be touch and go against those shitkickers from Upper Medlock as it is."

Marchbank wasn't wrong. At full-strength, or, as Penrose had once said in an honest if cutting assessment of the Lower Medlock team's abilities, full-weakness, they could just about hold their own against Upper Medlock. Over the past six years both villages had each posted three victories. All but the last of the matches had been close run things and the one that hadn't had been won more by subterfuge than by skill. If Lower Medlock had possessed a bowler with anything approaching the capabilities of Upper Medlock's Wayne Gibbon along with a batsman with the ability of their Piggy Higginbottom it would have been no contest, they would have won the games in a canter. But they didn't. What they did have were eleven players - if they were lucky - who could all bat and bowl a bit. Each and every batsman in the current team had scored a half century; a couple of them had even amassed centuries. Each and every bowler had taken five wickets; one of them had once achieved a hat-trick. The problem was that none of them ever did it in the same match, and usually not at all. To a man, and on one occasion, when they were two men short, a woman masquerading as a man, they habitually accumulated scores of anything from nought to twenty, but rarely any more, and returned bowling figures of no better than 2 for 40. Consequently they currently won very few matches against any opposition, let alone Upper Medlock.

At the beginning of the current season Marchbank, fully awake to his side's batting and bowling inconsistencies, and by this time aware that enthusiasm and countless sessions of bowling and batting practice in the nets were no substitute for talent, had decided that the way forward was for the team to improve its fielding technique, the intention being to cut down the opposing team's run count and therefore give the Lower Medlock side an increased chance of bettering it. A catching cradle, a device constructed of a tubular metal frame supporting rows of concave bamboo slats which, when a cricket ball is hurled at it, throws the ball off at various angles and at a catchable height, was purchased. A first practice session was organised immediately. Encouragingly, all thirteen players currently on the club's books turned up. At the second session, called for the following night, only nine of them turned up, three having had to cry off: Flatley, the local vet, because he was called out by a farmer to attend a cow that was having difficulty delivering of its calf; de la Mare, a merchant banker, who at the first session had fallen foul of the catching cradle which, far from improving his fielding technique had but paid to it for some time, along with his bowling and batting techniques, when he had almost been brained by a cricket ball flying off the frame at an unexpected angle and at a velocity approaching the speed of sound and hitting him between the eyes, pole-axing him and putting him in the local cottage hospital for a week; and Sneed, a financial adviser, who, realising that it could just as easily have been he who had ended up in hospital, had displayed precisely the same flaw in his character that had persuaded him take up his chosen profession and had said "Sod this for a game of soldiers," taken his leave and wasn't seen within a hundred yards of the ground for the next two months. The following week Marchbank himself had been struck painfully on the temple. In a show of bravado, and to set an example to the rest of the team, he had merely shook his head to clear it and carried on. However the blow had left him with double vision and when Penrose threw the ball hard onto the cradle the captain saw two balls careering off it in his direction and caught the wrong one. The right one cracked him painfully on the knee and put him out of action for the first two matches of the season. At that point the attempt to improve the team's fielding had been called off before more casualties could deplete the squad further.

"I'm afraid the pan-fried supreme of local chicken is off, sir," said the waiter, bending over to impart this sad news in Marchbank's ear.

"What?" Marchbank had only half heard the waiter, his mind still on the shitkickers from Upper Medlock and how it would be the arses of the Lower Medlock cricket team that would be kicked if they turned up to the match with less than a full complement of players.

"The pan-fried local chicken, sir. It's off." It wasn't, but the waiter was determined that Marchbank wasn't having any of it that evening. It was either that or spit on it sometime during its journey from pan to table, always a disgruntled waiter's option. However on this occasion he had decided against the ultimate reprisal, but only because he would be exacting revenge on Marchbank in the forthcoming derby match with Lower Medlock: the waiter was part of the Medlock bowling attack, a bowler whose technique was very fast but very erratic; fully aware of his waywardness he planned to pitch the ball in Marchbank's blockhole and about a yard wide of the wicket which, unless he had magically acquired the bowling skills of James Anderson since he had last performed, would probably hit his nemesis somewhere on his body from the chest upwards. He was hoping for the throat. "And the chef says to tell you you'll be able to have it fried in a coal bucket from next week," he concluded with a smile.

Marchbank treated the waiter to a withering glare. "Oh does he? Well you can tell the chef to piss off. And you can piss off too; I've got more important things to concern myself with than pan-fried fucking local fucking chicken."

"Your cricket match against Upper Medlock of course," said Paula Roderick with an understanding smile, trying to be sympathetic to Marchbank in his troubles.

Marchbank transferred his withering glare to her and ratcheted it up a couple of notches. "Well of course the bloody cricket match, what do you think, a game of hopscotch?"

"Only I was just thinking," Paula said, ignoring his outburst. "Why don't you get....whoseit to play for you?"

"Whoseit?"

"Whatsisname?"

"Well I don't know what his bloody name is do I, woman? It's you who's talking about whoever it is you're talking about."

The name suddenly came to Paula. "Jonny Pickering."

"Jonny Pickering?"

"That's the chap."

"You mean *the* Jonny Pickering. The former England cricketer? Retired not long back?"

"That's the one."

Marchbank sat back in his chair and regarded Paula for a moment. To fool her into thinking she had wormed her way into his good books with her suggestion he put on a pleased smile. "What a truly excellent idea, Paula." Having softened her up he treated her to a volley of his very best sarcasm. "I'll ask Ian Botham as well. And Freddy Flintoff, while I'm about it. Maybe Darren Gough too. I'm sure they'll all be only too happy to help us out."

It was completely wasted on Paula of course, who wouldn't have known an ex-England cricket star from a Taliban terrorist. In all innocence she said, "Have they come to live in Lower Medlock too?"

"What?"

"Like....what's he called, Jonny Pickering?"

Marchbank's jaw dropped, his mouth fell open and his eyes all but leapt out of their sockets. "Jonny Pickering has moved to Lower Medlock?"

"Into The Olde Mill Cottage to be precise. Grace Caldicott recognised him. Although for my part I wouldn't have known the man from Adam. We drove past in the car this afternoon when he was moving in. Grace stopped and got his autograph for Benjamin and Benedict. She said he was quite charming, quite the gentleman."

Marchbank clasped his hands together in prayer and looked towards heaven. "Oh thank you, God, thank you."

CHAPTER FOUR

The Brothers Grimm Affair

In 1961 Lower Medlock won the annual fixture with Upper Medlock for the fourth time in a row. It came as no surprise to either side; Lower Medlock had a much stronger team at the time, good enough win the West Medfordshire Conference for the past two seasons. Despite the Lower Medlock victories, all but one of them with quite a bit to spare, Upper Medlock had by far the best cricketer: Jim Grimm was a quite brilliant batsman who could have played the game at a much higher level should he have wished. His average in the East Medfordshire Conference that year was 86 and he wasn't far short of that figure in the previous three seasons; his lowest score during that entire period was 48 and he had amassed no less than twenty three centuries. If Upper Medlock had boasted another batsman half as good a Jim Grimm it would almost certainly have been all that was needed to tip the balance in their favour. But they didn't; and although their bowling was not far short of the standard of their opponents the remainder of their batting was woefully weak.

  Consequently they were always on the lookout for new

blood to boost their batting strength; but never with much luck. A couple of years previously they thought their fortunes had changed when a sunny-natured Jamaican, Eldred Wilkins, came to live in the village. On the Saturday following his arrival he went along to watch the cricket. Following the match, after introducing himself to the team, he asked the captain if they could perhaps give him a game, adding that they wouldn't have to provide him with a cricket bat as he had brought his own faithful bat with him from the West Indies. *Could they give him a game? A Jamaican who had taken the trouble to bring his own bat with him all the way from the West Indies? A Jamaican with a 'W' surname? Just let anybody try to stop them giving him a game!* The era of the great West Indies side that included the world famous 'Three Ws', Worrell, Weekes and Walcott, was still fresh in the memory, a time when it seemed that all West Indians were born with a cricket bat in one hand and a ball in the other. Even the current West Indies side, under the magnificent Gary Sobers, was second only to the Australians. Unfortunately Eldred Wilkins turned out to be about a hundred and second only to the Austrians, let alone the Australians, and after four matches, in which his total score with the bat was 0, he was never picked again, sunny-natured W-surnamed Jamaican or no.

On another occasion it again looked as though Upper Medlock's luck had changed when another foreigner came to live in the village, this one a go-getting ebullient New York American, posted to his petrochemical company's English branch as the firm's head trouble-shooter. After watching a match he had asked if he could try out for "Your quaint little old game of crocket" as it was "quite a bit like baseball and I was once good enough at the ball game to be considered for the Yankees, no less'. His request was granted on the 'any port in a storm' principal. To the delight of the Lower Medlock team he showed as much promise at crocket as he must have done at baseball, but before he could completely rid himself of the habit of flinging down the bat and setting off for square leg every time he connected with the ball he had moved back out of the village because he couldn't stand any more of the peace and quiet.

Harold Edmondson, a stalwart of the current Upper Medlock team, was lamenting this inability to recruit another decent batsman to team mate Jeff Slingsby in the queue at *Chippy's Plaice* fish and chip shop one Friday evening shortly before the next annual fixture.

"If only Joe Grimm played cricket too," he said, picturing this happy ideal in his mind before dismissing it with a sad shake of his head.

Slingsby concurred. "And as good as their Jim does."

"Even if he was only half as good as Jim."

"Them Lower Medlock buggers would have to watch out then, by hell would they!"

Edmondson had a thought which brought a hurt look to his face. "Do you know what one of the lads heard one of the wankers saying in *The Dun Cow* last week?"

"I wouldn't put anything past that load of tossers."

"That they wouldn't be surprised if we turned up this year waving a white flag."

"Crowing bastard."

The woman in front of them stepped to one side to salt and vinegar her fish and chips on the counter top and Slingsby stepped forward to take her place at the counter.

"You'd think they'd be alike, brothers, wouldn't you?" Edmondson mused, returning to his previous subject

"Fish, chips and peas please, Doris" said Slingsby to

the woman behind the counter.

"Same for me, Doris," said Edmondson, then said to Slingsby, "Identical twin brothers especially." He gave a deep sigh. "Not where the Grimm brothers are concerned apparently."

"Has Joe never played?"

"Not to my knowledge. Not even as a young lad. More interested in fishing as I remember; he was never away from the river with a rod."

They contemplated cricket's loss of Joe Grimm to angling while they were served their fish and chips. On the way out of the shop Slingsby suddenly stopped in thought. He said tentatively, still short of all the nuts and bolts of the idea that was forming in his mind, "He *could* play you know."

"Who play what?" said Edmondson vaguely, his attention now firmly on the consumption of his fish supper.

"Joe Grimm. He could play for us. He could be another Jim Grimm."

Edmondson shook his head as he popped a chip into his mouth. "Joe doesn't play cricket. I thought I'd already said that?"

"He doesn't have to." Slingsby gave a smile as more nuts and bolts arrived. "Well not in the usual way."

"What do you mean, not in the usual way?"

What Slingsby meant was that when the Upper Medlock side was fielding Joe Grimm would take his place in the field along with his identical twin Jim and the rest of the side, but when they were batting Jim would bat twice, the first time as himself, the second time as Joe.

It was perfect; it would be the easiest thing in the world to pull off Slingsby told the rest of the side in the cricket pavilion after the following Wednesday night's practice session. It couldn't be simpler. Jim would open the batting as usual. When he was out he would return to the crease as Joe following the fall of the next wicket. What was there to go wrong? One of the team pointed out that as Joe had never played cricket in his life he might be something of a liability in the field but another countered this by saying that they could afford the loss of a few runs and the odd missed catch if they were getting an average of another eighty odd runs in exchange for it. Apart from that, Edmondson added, if Joe was having a particularly bad time of it in the field he could pretend he'd twisted his ankle or hurt his back or something and had to leave the field, to be replaced by the twelfth man, who would field for the rest of the innings. The following day Joe was approached. He agreed to go along with the subterfuge, the payment of a fiver compensation for missing out on his Saturday afternoon's fishing was negotiated and agreed upon, and two weeks later he made the first of his four appearances in the annual fixture.

It went even better than expected. Upper Medlock batted first. Jim Grimm opened the batting as usual and, maybe freed up a little by the thought that his innings wasn't quite as critical to the team's success as it had previously been, punished the Lower Medlock bowling for 132 before being caught on the boundary in attempting a third six in a row. Ten minutes later, following the fall of the fifth wicket, he came in again as Joe, and with his eye already in made 80 in fifty minutes out of a total of 282 all out. This proved to be beyond the reach of the opposition who were all out for 224.

There were one or two remarks from the Lower Medlock players such as "Where have you been hiding *him*?" and "I didn't even know Jim Grimm had a twin brother", but nothing that might point to anyone harbouring suspicions that something untoward had taken place.

However the following year's fixture left quite a few of them harbouring suspicions when, after failing to take part in a single match for Upper Medlock during their league season, Joe turned out for them in the match against Lower Medlock and scored 87 in a winning total of 240 (Jim Grimm 92). What fuelled their scepticism was the fact that after just five overs of the Lower Medlock innings Joe, who during this time had let two balls that he should have stopped go for four and dropped an easy catch, had then left the field with an ankle injury that no one could remember seeing him sustain.

However it wasn't until the third meeting in which Joe took part that the Lower Medlock team had their suspicions confirmed. Again Jim Grimm posted an excellent knock of 72 before being run out. In attempting to gain the crease before the fielder's throw hit the wicket he slid into it feet first. The cricket field, having been subjected to a lot of rain that week, was quite green. Consequentially when Jim got to his feet he had a large grass stain on the left leg of his trousers. No one on the Lower Medlock side took much notice of this, clothing stained by grass being a regular occurrence in cricket; indeed several of them had grass stains on their clothing from their own exertions in the field. However their wicketkeeper Garforth took a lot of notice when Joe Grimm came out to bat with exactly the same grass stain on his trousers that his brother Jim had departed with five minutes earlier. Garforth took no time in calling the attention of his captain, Carstairs, to the coincidence, following which all hell broke loose. Accusations of cheating flew right, left and centre. Denials of cheating kept pace with them. Joe Grimm was asked why he had a grass stain on his trousers, bearing in mind it was the first time he'd been on the field of play that day, Upper

Medlock having won the toss and chosen to bat first. Grimm claimed that he had slipped and fallen to the ground on his way to the crease. Carstairs told him to tell them another one. Grimm couldn't think of another one so stuck firmly to his guns. Beside himself with rage Carstairs approached the umpires and told them he had reason to believe that the batsman at the crease was not Joe Grimm but Jim Grimm, and that Joe Grimm was probably hiding back in the pavilion, and gave his reasons for believing this. The umpires consulted and ruled that the only way to settle it was for the other Grimm twin to join them in the middle - if his trousers bore a similar grass stain then he was Jim Grimm, if they didn't he was Joe Grimm. Umpire Gearing returned to the pavilion accompanied by Carstairs and informed the Upper Medlock captain Edmondson that he would like to see the other brother Grimm, and the reason why. Alarmed, Edmondson said the first thing that came into his head, which was "Fuck me!" Then, maybe suspecting that this might be an inadequate response, said the second thing that came into his head, which was that following his innings Jim Grimm had been struck by a migraine and was lying down in the darkness of the dressing room and mustn't be disturbed for whatever reason. Carstairs told Edmondson that Grimm would be struck by more than a migraine if he didn't show his face within the next five seconds, he would be struck by a cricket bat, and bloody hard. Thinking on his feet Slingsby said that whilst it was untrue that Jim Grimm was in the dressing room it was true that he had contracted a migraine, indeed a migraine of such severe proportions that he had had to go home, where he could lie down in his bedroom with the curtains drawn, and would therefore be taking no further part in the match.

Carstairs had no alternative but to accept this unlikely story but was far from being a happy bunny, as were the rest of the Lower Medlock players. Especially after Jim Grimm as Joe Grimm performed even more brilliantly than usual and was largely responsible in building a match-winning total of 247.

Jim Grimm might have continued to bat both as himself and his brother for many years to come. However fate stepped in when Lower Medlock's vice-captain Clive Hornchurch's wife Clarissa set fire to the chip pan.

Hornchurch had never seen the Combined Upper and Lower Medlock Fire Service in action before and was surprised to see one of the Grimm brothers amongst its firemen. He wondered idly if it was Jim or Joe but certainly had no agenda when, after the fire had been safely extinguished and he had thanked the firemen, he asked Grimm which of the brothers he was. "I'm Joe," the Grimm brother had replied with a friendly smile. From somewhere in the back of his mind Hornchurch recalled that Joe was the gardener he had employed to re-lay his front lawn several years previously. He asked him if he'd given up gardening in exchange for a career in the fire service. Joe explained that he was still a full-time gardener but in addition was a part-time, auxiliary fireman. Hornchurch had thought no more about it, then one Saturday evening a few weeks later following a league fixture, the subject of the forthcoming match with Lower Medlock came up and an opinion voiced that the cheating bastards would probably try to get away with the Grimm brothers con again. The consensus was that they almost certainly would, as it was the only chance they had of winning. All present were asked by Carstairs if they had any ideas as to how they could stop Lower Medlock getting away with it again, but it was a question he had asked frequently before and as before no one came up with a solution.

It was only when he was getting into bed that night, just as the fire alarm went off, that the answer to the problem came to Hornchurch.

September 8 1962.

Upper Medlock v Lower Medlock. Wickets pitched 2pm. Umpires S Phillips, B Grogan.

Lower Medlock 193 all out.

Upper Medlock

Jim Grimm b Peebles 91
J Slingsby c Greaves b Archibald 2
F Wilson and b Cheapside 11
H A L Edmondson (C) b Cheapside 33
P Hibbert st Harris b Peebles 0
O Brookes run out 1
J Johnson c Hornchurch b Stubbs 12
L P Burnett b Peebles 2
W Wood c Harris b Cheapside 3
W Waverley b Archibald 0
Joe Grimm did not bat.
  Extras 12
    Total 167

Lower Medlock won by 26 runs.

All was going to plan with Upper Medlock's reply to their

opponent's total of 193 until the dismissal of Jim Grimm at the fall of the fourth wicket. At that point it looked as though it might be a close run thing but with 127 already on the board and Joe Grimm to come in they were definitely in the box seat. However Joe Grimm didn't come in; that is Jim Grimm came in as Joe Grimm but only as far as stepping out through the pavilion door and making his way down the steps, at which juncture the fire alarm went off. Almost immediately Joe Grimm burst first out of the dressing room, then out of the pavilion and down the steps, almost knocking his brother over in his rush to get to the fire.

But there was no fire of course.

Three weeks earlier when the fire alarm had gone off it had dawned on Hornchurch that if it happened to go off during the cricket match then Joe Grimm, as an auxiliary fireman, would be duty bound to attend the fire. He did a little research and found this to be the case. His investigations also informed him that the routine followed by the Combined Upper and Lower Medlock Fire Service, once the fire alarm had sounded, was for the four auxiliary firemen to make their way with all haste to the assembly point outside the Lower Medlock village hall, from whence they would be picked up by the two full-time firemen manning the fire engine, and thence on to the fire. All it would take, Hornchurch had realised, was a 999 fire call at the appropriate time, and the rest, as they say, would be history. Along with Joe Grimm's successful career with Upper Medlock.

And so it proved to be.

CHAPTER FIVE

French Cut
1. Any poorly executed shot that results in an inside edge which narrowly misses hitting the stumps.
2. A canal in France.

Persuading Jonny Pickering to turn out for Lower Medlock had been easier than Marchbank could have hoped for even in his wildest dreams. Pickering would be honoured to play for the village. Furthermore, not only would he be delighted to turn out for them in the annual match against Upper Medlock but he would also turn out for them every Saturday in their league games in the West Medfordshire Conference. Was the ex-England star and Ashes hero in good nick, Marchbank wanted to know - he certainly looked as though he was? Pickering informed him that he couldn't have felt better, as fit as a butcher's dog, just raring to go. Had he played much cricket since retiring from the first class scene? No, but it hadn't been all that long since he'd been in action and he was sure he would acquit himself to Marchbank's satisfaction. Marchbank positively glowed.

And Pickering was so affable, so very-good natured, a really fine fellow. Marchbank, a keen follower of cricket at the very top level in addition to being a participant of it at the very bottom level, hadn't been surprised; he had read in the newspapers that Pickering had an agreeable personality. However as a member of the legal profession, and therefore distrustful of anything that moved and most things that didn't, especially anything in the newspapers - organs that would no doubt just be paying him lip service to suit their own purposes, if Marchbank knew anything about them - he had taken such reports with a large pinch of salt. He had also seen Pickering interviewed on *The Jonathan Ross Show* on television, where he had come across as the perfect gentleman, but this too was not conclusive proof to Marchbank's way of thinking, the Lower Medlock captain being of the opinion that a man appearing as a guest on one of the nation's leading chat shows is not going to make much of an effort to come across as a twat. Besides, that role is adequately filled by the host.

But Pickering had turned out to be everything the newspapers had claimed him to be, had been exactly as he had appeared to be in his cosy up with Wossie. Chancing his arm, Marchbank had mentioned to Pickering that he could turn out for Lower Medlock in their match against the neighbouring village of Slocombe that coming Saturday, if he wished. However Pickering had declined, saying that he wouldn't even dream of taking the place of someone who had already been selected. He would, however, come along to watch, to give them his support, if he may. If he may! Marchbank's cup ranneth over.

Both Marchbank and Roderick, who had accompanied his captain to The Olde Mill Cottage, had been hopeful rather than confident that they would get their man. There were, after all, many reasons why they wouldn't - Pickering wasn't interested in playing at a lower level, he was far too busy doing other things, he had an old injury that might start playing up and he didn't dare risk it, he wanted to spend more time with his family - and not a single reason why he would, so far as they could see. But joy of joys he *did* want to play for them; he had nothing else on, he had no injuries, and he had no wife and children to stake a claim on his Saturday afternoons; there was nothing to stop him playing for them.

For Pickering's part an amiable Saturday afternoon knock seemed to be just the ticket, just what the doctor ordered. In fact it *was* what the doctor had ordered, more or less. Keen not to give up cricket altogether, but fearful of bringing on another stroke, perhaps a more serious one the next time, he had sought Dr Purseglove's advice on the matter. It would be very low level stuff, he had explained, village cricket at most, nothing too serious. Happily the doctor had told him that not only could he play village cricket but that he wholeheartedly recommended it; a nice relaxing game could only help to remove any worries that might still be dwelling on his mind.

Pickering also felt that playing cricket for the village side would help integrate him into the community, something he was keen to do. Although he had chosen to live in the depths of the country it didn't mean that he wished to become a recluse; far from it, he wanted to take a full part in village life. This aspiration had only been bolstered by the character of the men who had called on him that morning and invited him to play for their cricket team, the men who had taken the trouble to come along to his new home to welcome him to their village less than twenty-four hours after he had moved into it, who seemed to be just the sort of four square men with whom he wished to become associated and better acquainted with.

"Can I top you up, Jerry?" he now asked, picking up the bottle of excellent burgundy he had opened shortly after his visitors had arrived.

"Don't mind if I do, Jonny, don't mind if I do," said Marchbank, holding out his almost empty wine glass.

Marchbank had been a little concerned when Pickering had produced the bottle of *Nuit-St- Georges*, for it was only ten minutes past nine that Saturday morning - Roderick had doubted the wisdom of such an early call to someone who had moved into his new home only the day before but Marchbank had insisted that he wanted to strike while the iron was hot - and whilst it was wonderful that Pickering had agreed to play for them it wouldn't be quite so wonderful if he turned up to play pissed out of his skull, as someone who apparently thought nothing of cracking open a bottle at that time in the morning might be prone to do. However on gently hinting to Pickering that it was maybe a little early to be imbibing the ex-England skipper had said that the bottle was in the way of celebrating their new friendship, and that he only ever drank to be sociable.

*

At exactly the same time Pickering was topping up the glasses of his new friends Duckworth and Bristow turned off the main road between the two Medlock villages and into the narrow road that led up to The Olde Mill Cottage. Just as Marchbank had no doubts that the cottage was in Lower Medlock Duckworth had no doubts that it was in Upper Medlock. Neither man, nor any of their team mates, had even considered it might be in the others' village. But why would they? Positioned as it was, on the outer edge and northernmost point of both villages, it was an easy assumption to make. Not one of them had even been born when the controversy over which village and in which county the cottage stood following the boundary change in 1962, and by now the affair was lost in the mists of time.

"My back's playing up again," said Duckworth, feeling a familiar twinge as he stepped aside to avoid a large lichen-encrusted stone that had detached itself from the dry-stone wall bordering the road.

"Oh yes?" said Bristow.

"The doctor says to rest it. Bloody idiot. How the hell are you supposed to rest your back when you're a window cleaner?"

"Not easy, Les."

"Anyway I took a week off last week but it didn't make any difference."

"These doctors know nothing."

"Then he suggested a body belt might help."

"*The Godfather's* on telly again tonight; great film *The Godfather*."

Marchbank looked sharply at Bristow but didn't break stride.

They carried on in silence for a minute or so before turning into the lane that led to The Olde Mill Cottage's front door.

"Nice house," said Duckworth, when the cottage came into view.

"Been empty for nearly twelve months."

"Bit isolated though. For my taste."

"They don't come much more isolated."

"Nice though." Duckworth avoided another fallen wall stone. "I wonder how much a house like that would set you back?"

"I'm thinking of going down to the Cotswolds for a

few days next week if I can get our Arthur to do my round."

Duckworth pulled up sharply, pulling Bristow up with him.

"Why have we stopped?" said Bristow.

"When we get there let me do the talking," said Duckworth firmly.

"What?"

"About Pickering turning out for us. Let me do all the talking."

"Why?"

"Because you'll keep changing the subject and confuse everything."

"I won't."

"Yes you will; you always do, you do it all the time."

"I don't."

"Yes you do, you did it just then."

"When?"

"When we were talking about the cottage and then you started talking about going to the Cotswolds. And before that when I was talking about my bad back and you started talking about *The Godfather*. You do it all the time; you do it so often you don't even know you're doing it. We'll never get anywhere. I can just imagine it: *Me:* If you like, Jonny, you can be captain. *Jonny:* Well what would the others think about that? *You:* I'm thinking of going to see the Lions of Longleat next week." Duckworth shook his head. "I mean he's going to be confused enough as it is what with you being dressed as a milkman."

"I *am* a milkman."

"He'll probably think we've come to flog him a bottle of gold top."

"That isn't *my* fault."

"You *had* to wear a peaked cap and a striped apron then?"

"Well I'm in the middle of my round, aren't I."

Duckworth gave in, unable to fault Bristow's logic. He would far rather have approached Pickering on his own but Bristow had insisted that as vice-captain it was only right and proper that he be involved. Duckworth had only agreed under suffrage and because the last time he had refused to allow Bristow to accompany him on club business the vice-captain had left him without milk for a week in reprisal. As this had entailed Mrs Duckworth having to walk up the hill to Ahmed's Convenience Store every day to get some, an additional chore that hadn't gone down at all well with her, it was not something that he wanted to chance happening again. "Well just let me do all the talking," he said.

"I'm not just standing there like a spare prick at a wedding," Bristow protested.

"Well don't keep changing the subject then."

Their conversation had delivered them to The Olde Mill Cottage's front door. Duckworth rang the doorbell. "Stand well to one side when he comes to the door," he warned. "Preferably out of sight completely."

"Why?"

"Because we want him telling us he'll play for Upper Medlock, not that he'd like a bottle of milk every day and a strawberry yoghurt on Fridays," said Duckworth impatiently. "So just do it will you."

*

On hearing the doorbell Jonny Pickering cocked an ear. "Hello? My word I *am* popular this morning." He put down his glass of wine on the coffee table and got to his feet. "Excuse me a moment would you, gentlemen."

"But of course, Jonny," said Marchbank.

"Yes?" smiled Pickering, opening the front door a moment or two later.

"We're not after your milk order," said Duckworth quickly. Although Bristow had reluctantly stood to one side he hadn't made much of an effort and was still clearly visible to Pickering. "We're here on a completely different, non-milk matter."

"Oh?"

"Yes. We would like...."

"Although I would be only too happy to add you to my round, Mr Pickering," said Bristow.

"I see."

"In fact it would be my pleasure. In addition to milk - full cream semi-skimmed and skimmed - I do yoghurt, eggs, an excellent farmhouse cheddar...."

Cutting his colleague off short, Duckworth turned to him, Oliver Hardy to Bristow's Stan Laurel, fixed him with a look of pity, shook his head sadly and said, "Now what did I just say?"

"What?"

"About you changing the subject?"

"I was only telling him what I carry as well as...."

"You were *changing* the fucking *subject*." Duckworth turned to Pickering, embarrassed at his use of the f-word and Bristow's merchandising in equal measure. "Sorry about that, Mr Pickering. The...."

"No, it's all right, I understand," Pickering said with a charming smile. Then to Bristow he said, "Put me down for a pint of semi-skimmed daily and a dozen eggs every Friday."

"That's very good of you, Mr Pickering, if I may say so, very good indeed."

"Jonny. I insist you call me Jonny."

"Jonny. They're new laid and free range of course, Jonny, the eggs. And how about some farmhouse cheddar? Very nutty, comes in one pound blocks?"

"I'll take a pound once a week."

Duckworth looked at Bristow with a look that said if he didn't shut up, and quick, he might very well end up with a pound of his nutty farmhouse cheddar where the sun doesn't shine, but said to him, with an exaggerated show of patience, "Have you *quite* finished?"

Bristow hadn't. "Yoghurt, Jonny?"

Pickering wrinkled his nose. "Not keen on yoghurt I'm afraid."

"Cream?"

"Oh for fuck's sake," said Duckworth, screwing up his eyes and clutching the lank hair at the sides of head in frustration. This time, without bothering to apologise for his use of the f-word again, possibly thinking it was fully justified, he said, "Sorry, Mr Pickering, it's just...."

"Jonny. Everyone calls me Jonny."

"Jonny. It's just that I'm eager, very eager, to know if you'll turn out for our cricket team?"

Pickering's eyebrows raised in surprise. "More of you? My, you *are* keen to get me on board."

"What?"

"I mean I've already been asked. I've got two of your team mates with me at this very moment."

It can only be Francis and Spragg, thought Duckworth; Gibbon had said he was going to a *Flog It!* valuation at Crewe. He would have to be having a strict word with his team mates the next time he saw them, he could see; after all it was he who was captain; it was up to the captain and no one else to ask Jonny Pickering if he would play for them.

"In fact we're just having a celebratory glass of wine to seal my acceptance," said Pickering. "Come in and join us, do. I'm sure I'll be able to lay my hands on another bottle somewhere." He stood aside and with an exaggerated sweep of his arm invited them to step right inside. "After you, gentlemen."

When Pickering led them into the living room it was a toss-up who was more surprised, the members of the Upper Medlock team or those from Lower Medlock, but both were probably more surprised than Lazarus had been when he discovered that he was alive and kicking again.

Marchbank glowered at Duckworth. "What the devil are you two doing here?"

"I could ask you the same thing," said Duckworth, matching Marchbank's glower.

"Not that it's any of your damn business, but we've invited Jonny to play for us."

"What's more he has agreed," added Roderick, with a fawning smile at Pickering.

Duckworth dismissed this out of hand. "He can't play for you, he lives in Upper Medlock."

"The hell he does," said Marchbank. "He lives in Lower Medlock."

"Oh yes?" countered Duckworth. "And how exactly do you make that out?"

In 1951, after the Medlock cricket team had divided itself into two teams, some of the players who lived in Upper Medlock had initially turned out for Lower Medlock and vice versa. No one thought this odd; it came about mostly because of long-standing friendships between members who simply wanted to carry on playing their cricket with their mates. This was far from being the case in 2013.

Despite the events of 1962, during the match that came to be known as *The Brothers Grimm Affair*, and the events of 1968, known thereafter as *The Church Clock Affair*, it wasn't until the1974 fixture, thanks to the encounter that came to be known as *The Dr Hodgkinson Affair*, that residents of one village ceased to play for the team of the other village. The flames were further fanned in 1983 when, after losing three games on the trot, Lower Medlock brought in a ringer - a top class all-rounder from Yorkshire - to ensure that the losing sequence didn't stretch to a fourth defeat. The match came to be known as *The Yorkshire Ringer Affair*, and in order to guarantee, at the insistence of Upper Medlock, that such a thing could never be repeated, it was agreed that from then on only men born in, or currently domiciled in, their particular village, could take part. By 1989, after what came to be known as *The Space Cake Affair,* relations between the two villages had further deteriorated and by 2003, following the game that came to be known as *The Piggy Higginbottom Affair,* what had once been friendly rivalry had progressed through dislike into outright revulsion. By 2011, in what became known as *The Flog It! Affair,* it had developed into downright all-encompassing hate.

"The Olde Mill Cottage has *always* been in Lower Medlock," said Marchbank, absolutely convinced that he was right.

"Wrong. It has *always* been in Upper Medlock," said Duckworth with equal conviction.

"There is not a shadow of doubt that the cottage is in Lower Medlock," said Roderick.

"Do any of you know a good plumber?" said Bristow. "Only my boiler's on the blink."

Marchbank, wondering what Bristow's boiler had to do with it and suspecting that mention of it might be some sort of trick to sidetrack him disregarded the milkman and said to Duckworth dismissively, "So I would appreciate it if you and your pet monkey made yourself scarce." He glanced at Pickering before continuing. "And I'm sure I speak for Jonny."

Pickering's expression indicated that he wasn't as sure about this as Marchbank but before he could say anything Duckworth said, "I'll make *you* bloody scarce," and rolling up his sleeves took a threatening step towards Marchbank.

Marchbank stood his ground and said aloofly, "The threat of violence is all I would expect from the pond-life that passes for humanity in Upper Medlock."

"It isn't a threat it's a promise, you toffee-nosed tosser," said Duckworth, taking a further step towards Marchbank, at the same time drawing back his arm and balling his hand into a fist.

Pickering quickly stepped between the two. "Now hold on, please, gentlemen. I'm sure this can all be sorted out quite amicably."

Jonny Pickering did not know the villages and villagers of Upper Medlock and Lower Medlock or he would never have made such a statement. He especially didn't know the members of their respective cricket teams, of whom the expression amicable would have been about as appropriate had it been used to describe the atmosphere between Anne Boleyn and Henry the Eighth the day before the executioner chopped Anne's head off. And, whilst there was history between the two sides, there was history of Winston Churchill and Adolf Hitler proportions between their respective captains. Leaving aside the cricket situation, Marchbank had not only summarily dismissed Duckworth from the job of cleaning his windows, following an incident involving his wife Bethany, but had persuaded the rest of the Lower Medlock team and a considerable number of their many supporters to do likewise.

At the time of the incident Marchbank hadn't even been aware that Duckworth was the man who cleaned his windows every Monday morning - he would have preferred the Devil himself, given the choice - as he left that sort of thing to Bethany. He discovered it on his return home from the office the day Duckworth had suddenly appeared outside the Marchbanks' master bedroom when Bethany was towelling herself dry following her morning shower, the apparition at the window causing her to scream out and drop the towel to the floor in surprise. Whether it was a natural reaction to Bethany's scream, as Duckworth claimed, or to get a better perspective on her naked charms, as Marchbank claimed, was not clear, but at that point Duckworth took a step backwards; not the wisest of moves when one is perched at the top of a ladder. The upshot was that in falling to the ground Duckworth injured his back quite severely, an injury that put him out of commission for several weeks, at least so far as cleaning windows was concerned. It did not however stop him from seeking legal advice, and a week later a letter from Needham & Needham, Solicitors, Middleham, arrived in Marchbank's post, informing him that on behalf of their client Leslie George Duckworth, of 22 Steeple End Fold, Upper Medlock, they would be suing for damages and loss of income. Marchbank's response was to inform Needham & Needham that if the frivolous and totally unsubstantiated claim was not withdrawn forthwith that *he* would be suing Duckworth for voyeurism. Duckworth sued, Marchbank counter-sued, and the case is still going on to this day.

Now, in response to Duckworth calling him a toffee-nosed tosser, Marchbank said, "Sticks and stones may break my bones but names will never hurt me," at the same time raising his fists to defend himself in case Duckworth wasn't content with just calling him names and took it upon himself to implement the breaking bones part of the saying.

Which Duckworth immediately proceeded to do by shoving Pickering bodily to one side and throwing a haymaking right at his adversary. Leaning smartly to one side Marchbank just managed to evade the blow, and as Pickering tried to get between them again responded to Duckworth's attack with a haymaking right of his own. Bony fist crunched resoundingly into flesh and bone of eye. But unfortunately not Duckworth's, Jonny Pickering's. A split second later Duckworth's second attempt to land one on Marchbank struck Pickering a severe blow in his other eye, causing a similarly sickening, crunching sound.

CHAPTER SIX

The Church Clock Affair

Following *The Brothers Grimm Affair* it took quite some time for the members of the Upper and Lower Medlock teams to regard one another with anything but deep distrust; however by 1968 their wounds had healed sufficiently for them to at least get through their annual fixture without a fight breaking out. Since the affair both teams had been victorious on three occasions, Upper Medlock finally having been successful in improving their batting strength, this time legitimately, thanks to the addition to their ranks of Ralph Breeze and Gerald Shippon from the nearby village of Much Nettleton, whose cricket team had been dissolved after their ground had been subjected to a compulsory purchase order to make way for the new Middleham by-pass. There had been murmurings amongst the Lower Medlock players that the Middleham by-pass scheme and its subsequent compulsory purchase orders had been implemented with unusual speed, and that a possible reason for this was that one of the Upper Medlock team, Alex Clunes, was a county councillor, and as such was in a position to influence matters in this regard; however nothing could be proved.

So it was in a state of relative peace that the next fixture began.

September 2, 1968.

Upper Medlock v Lower Medlock. Wickets pitched 2pm. Umpires S Chesworth, A Morten.

Upper Medlock 210 all out.

Lower Medlock

J Gartside b Clunes 43
R L Breeze c Greaves b Smith 47
A Edmondson(C) lbw b Clunes 17
P Hibbert b Peebles 24
G B Shippon not out 41
The Rev A Hartley retired hurt 10
L Mason not out 15
  Extras 14
   Total 211 for 4

Lower Medlock won by 6 wickets.

The cricket ground at Lower Medlock is owned by St Matthew's Church, a handsome-looking Norman structure dating from the twelfth century. In its largesse, and very probably because the Vicar of Medlock was a founder member of the Medlock club when it was formed in 1888, the church allows the cricket team the use of the ground for a peppercorn rent of one penny per annum, but with one proviso: that not a ball shall be bowled, regardless of the state of play in the match, after 8 pm. This stipulation is set as deeply in stone as the inscriptions on the tombs and gravestones surrounding the church, many of them the final resting place of former cricketers, 'Out at last' and 'Not out, merely sleeping' being just two of their fanciful inscriptions. ('Bowled his last maiden over' had not been allowed following an objection by the local branch of the Women's Institute.) A further guarantee that the church's wishes would be adhered to was that the incumbent vicar would be a member of the Medlock club, and if not a playing member then a club official.

The 8 pm proviso had never caused a problem until the 1968 meeting. Until 1954, when the games were of unlimited overs, if the match was still undecided by eight-o-clock the game simply ended in a draw. After 1954, when the format changed to limited over and the matches decided over forty overs per side, there had always been sufficient time to complete the fixtures, or at least those fixtures that the English summer weather hadn't already put paid to by rain, and on a couple of occasions snow. In fact rainfall was to play no small part in the 1968 match, two lengthy showers being responsible for the loss of over an hour's play. This had the effect of putting Lower Medlock's reply to Upper Medlock's total of 210 well behind schedule if they were to have any hopes of getting the required runs before the clock struck eight. Some very tight bowling by Smith and Clunes - although thankfully the two bowlers weren't taking the wickets that might yield a victory for their side - put the Lower Medlock reply even further behind schedule, making a drawn game very much on the cards.

At this point there had been more than a suggestion that, with an eye on the clock, the Upper Medlock side had been purposely slowing things down - being somewhat dilatory in returning the ball back on the occasions it had been dispatched for a boundary, taking their time making the change in fielding positions at the end of each over, a bowler forever altering the position of his field in the middle of an over; in fact just the normal sort of gamesmanship one expects in a game of cricket, but no more than that. And certainly not near enough to justify the scandalous behaviour which was to follow.

At eight minutes to eight by the church clock - from which the umpires were duty bound by the church to take their timing - it was looking like a lost cause for the home side: twenty more runs were required but with few minutes to get them, and the bowling as tight as ever.

It was at this juncture that The Reverend Hartley, the current vicar of St Matthew's church, approached umpire Chesworth complaining of severe stomach pains: he thought he was running a temperature, it was all he could do to keep from vomiting, if he were to vomit he certainly didn't want to do it on the cricket pitch, heaven forbid, could he possibly be excused? Umpire Chesworth, after a brief consultation with Umpire Morten, ruled that the reverend could leave the field, retired hurt. The opposition's captain was informed and The Reverend Hartley left the field clutching his stomach rather dramatically, and perhaps a little too quickly for a man in severe pain, to be replaced by the next batsman, Mason.

All this had soaked up another three minutes and it was exactly five minutes to eight by the time the new batsman had taken guard and faced up to his first ball. He took a two from it, a handsome drive through the mid-wicket area, blocked the next delivery, and then, chancing his arm, hooked the final ball of the over for a four. This left fourteen runs required for victory, but with virtually no time left to get them. Shippon now faced Upper Medlock's best bowler,

Clunes. Perhaps inspired by his new batting partner's success Shippon hit out at the first delivery and despatched it through the covers to the boundary for another four. Could victory still be possible? Possible, yes, but even the most optimistic of the Lower Medlock team wouldn't have risked so much as a penny on it. It would have been a wise decision; Shippon's boundary proved to be a false dawn and it was his only success until the final ball of the over, which he edged through the slips down to third man for two.

Shawcross, the Upper Medlock captain, glanced up at the clock, confidently expecting the hands to show that there wouldn't be time for another over, probably not enough time to even start one. However, and to his surprise, the clock was registering two minutes to eight. Shawcross, aware that time sometimes has a nasty habit of standing still when you most want it to get a move on, put the discrepancy down to this phenomenon. However he wasn't at all worried, secure in the knowledge that by the time the fielders had changed positions in readiness for the next over there would be no more than a minute to go at the most, and Ted Dexter and Tom Graveney themselves weren't going to score fourteen runs in a minute, let alone the Lower Medlock batsmen, and a well-deserved victory would be Upper Medlock's. Therefore it came as something of a shock to him when he looked up at the church clock after Shippon had hit a four off the first ball of the new over to find that it still showed two minutes to eight. He blinked, rubbed his eyes and looked again, but the hands hadn't budged so much as a centimetre from when he'd last looked, at least two minutes ago. Those members of the Upper Medlock side who had also been keeping an eye on the minute hand of the clock were equally surprised on looking up and noting the time. The Lower Medlock batsmen were surprised. Umpires Chesworth and Morten were surprised. The eighty or so spectators were surprised. The only person not surprised, now high in the clock tower of the church, was The Reverend Hartley, the man responsible for stopping the clock.

Consternation replaced surprise on the faces of the Upper Medlock team. Hope replaced it on the faces of the Lower Medlock batsmen. Confusion replaced it on the faces of umpires Chesworth and Morten, both of whom were at a loss as to what to do. But, as Shippon was quick to point out to them, a proviso was a proviso, the law was the law, a deal was a deal, the clock had yet to strike eight. With nothing else for it Umpire Chesworth signalled for the game to continue and Shippon and Mason knocked off the runs. With two minutes to spare.

Only then did The Reverend Hartley remove the wooden plank he had jammed between the cogs of the clock's mechanism. As the ancient timepiece whirred into action again the reverend gave a benevolent smile, looked heavenwards in thanks to God, and made his way back down the spiral stone staircase to finish off writing his sermon for the morrow, 'Love Thy Neighbour'. He thought that Hymn number 559, *Lead us heavenly Father, lead us*, might chime rather well with it.

CHAPTER SEVEN

Flipper.
1. A leg spin delivery with under-spin, so that the ball bounces lower than it would normally.
2. A TV show about a dolphin.

"Apparently it's all to do with the brook; Blackbottom Brook," said Marchbank.

"What about it?" said Roderick.

On the Tuesday evening following their visit to The Olde Mill Cottage Marchbank and Roderick were back in *The Dun Cow* along with Penrose and three more of the Lower Medlock team. On this occasion they weren't in the restaurant but huddled together in a dark corner of the lounge bar - residents of Upper Medlock rarely ventured into *The Dun Cow*, if at all, but it was better to be on the safe side, walls having ears and such. Dark corners weren't difficult to find in The Dun Cow, in fact dark anywhere wasn't hard to find, the landlord keeping the whole pub in a constant state of semi-darkness as he fondly imagined it added to the ambience. In addition to the ambience it had also added a claim for damages from a man who had stumbled blindly into the furniture and bruised an arm in the resultant fall. However the landlord saw this as a small price to pay, and anyway the savings in electricity more than covered the £200 he had been forced to fork out.

The darkness in the corner in which the Lower Medlock party was huddled was especially dark. It mirrored Marchbank's mood. "It's a right balls-up and no mistake, according to that bloody clown Bleakley," he said, and went on to explain to the gathering what the bloody clown had explained to him in great and increasingly worrying detail.

Gerald Bleakley, not only Clerk to the Council of both villages but also the neighbouring village of Stonely - none of the villages being large enough to warrant the exclusive use of a Clerk to the Council - took his time in answering Marchbank's enquiry as to which of the two villages The Olde Mill Cottage was in. Chickens had come home to roost and he intended to make the most of it. He put on a smile, sat back in his leather chair and said pleasantly, "Oddly enough I was asked the same question by the captain of the Upper Medlock team."

"Duckworth?" Marchbank's eyes widened in shock and surprise. "Has Duckworth been here?"

"Tuesday morning, first thing. I'd hardly had chance to get behind my desk before he was badgering me. I told him precisely what I am about to tell you."

Having stated his intentions Bleakley seemed in no hurry to carry them out. Serenely he sat back and examined his nails as though this was part of the process. Marchbank, in more than a hurry, chivvied him along. "Well come on man, stop beating about the bush, some of us are busy men even if Clerks to the Council seem to have all day."

Bleakley smiled a deeply satisfied smile. "The Olde Mill Cottage is neither in Lower Medlock nor Upper Medlock."

Marchbank blinked. "What do you mean it's in neither

of them?"

"And yet it is in both of them."

"Both of them?"

"That is my understanding."

Marchbank's mood improved instantly. "Well I don't see how you make that out, but then nor am I particularly interested; if it is in both of them it means Jonny Pickering can play for us."

Bleakley's smile becoming more and more satisfied by the second he now deftly dropped the spanner in the works. *"Depending upon whether it is gas, electricity or water that is under discussion."*

"What?"

"Those are the utilities that are the criteria, I am led to believe."

"What criteria?"

"Whether The Olde Mill Cottage is situated in Lower Medlock or Upper Medlock."

"Gas, electricity or water?"

"That is my information."

Marchbank's brow furrowed. "What the hell have gas, electricity and water got to do with it?"

Bleakley was enjoying himself immensely. It was Marchbank, in his capacity as Deputy Chairman of the Lower Medlock Parish Council, who had been chiefly instrumental in restricting his last two annual salary increases to half of one per cent, blaming it on Government cutbacks. The Clerk's smile changed to a frown. "Not sure about cricket though." He considered it for a moment. "I suppose it would all depend."

"Depend? What would depend? And stop talking in bloody riddles."

Bleakley let Marchbank stew a little longer before answering. Eventually he said, "I am assuming, never having been there myself - golf's my game, for my sins - that you have a supply of water laid on in your cricket pavilion, and that the building is illuminated by electricity. If, however, your cooking equipment is powered by gas, that would place you in both camps. Then again, if you cook by electricity....?" Bleakley spread his hands as though if that state of affairs pertained then the matter was open to question, and left the sentence unfinished. Which was perhaps just as well as the cricket ground's utilities had nothing to do with it, and were just the Clerk's way of getting Marchbank even more confused than he already was. However, even if he had completed the sentence his words would have been drowned out by Marchbank, who jumped to his feet as though about to exact violence on Bleakley and bellowed, "If you don't stop fucking about and tell me what the fuck you're going on about, and do it without that stupid civil servants grin on your face, not only will you not get even half a per cent raise in salary this year but you will be looking for a fucking job."

Aware that he had gone as far as he could Bleakley put Marchbank fully in the picture regarding The Olde Mill Cottage.

Now, in *The Dun Cow*, Marchbank, having done the same for his team mates, said, "So I'm looking for ideas from any of you?"

"Well as I see it, if The Old Mill Cottage is in both villages Pickering can play for us," said Penrose. "I don't see a problem."

"The problem," said Marchbank patiently, "is that he can also play for Upper Medlock."

"Did he actually *say* he wouldn't play for us?" said

Archibald Doyle-Davidson, one of the Lower Medlock opening batsmen.

"He didn't say he'd play for either of us. He said he'd have to give it some thought. But if I'd given you a black eye would you play for us?"

"I thought you said Duckworth gave him a black eye too?"

"He did."

"Well it seems to me that we're even stevens on the black eye front, with all to play for," said Doyle-Davidson. He paused for a moment, considering his words before he went on. "As I see it we have merely to make his playing for Lower Medlock a more attractive proposition than his playing for Upper Medlock. Which shouldn't be beyond our wit."

Marchbank didn't feel anywhere near as optimistic. Gloomily he said, "Yes well that might be easier said than done. That twat of a milkman Bristow is already supplying Pickering with free milk and eggs and that even bigger twat of a window cleaner Duckworth is cleaning his windows for free."

"Why on earth would they offer their goods and services for free?" said Flatley, who as a solicitor probably didn't understand the concept of you scratch my back and I'll scratch yours.

"Well obviously to influence his choice of course," said Marchbank, a much trickier solicitor.

"Perhaps we too can supply him with something free?" said Penrose.

"Yes, good idea, maybe you can start the ball rolling by giving him your Barry Manilow ticket," said Marchbank.

"I thought I'd explained that," said Penrose with a hurt look.

Marchbank snorted. "It could never in a million years be explained to my satisfaction why attending a Barry Manilow concert is preferable to putting one across those mouth breathers from Upper Medlock."

"I'm afraid it could be worse than you think, Marchers," said first change bowler Giles Sturgess ominously.

Marchbank's head snapped round. "What do you mean, worse?"

"Bristow and Duckworth might not be the only ones making with the freebies; when I drove past the cottage in the hearse yesterday that painter fellow Spragg was giving the outside a new coat of whitewash."

"Shit!"

"Shit indeed."

"And that won't be the end of it if I know them," said Marchbank, becoming more depressed by the second.

"Doesn't one of them do a bit of thatching?" said Penrose, as though on cue.

"Scrivener," said Sturgess. "Tommy Scrivener. He used to make his living at it when there were a lot more thatched roofs around, not like today; but he'll still be able to do it."

"Pound to a pinch of shit he'll be re-thatching Pickering's roof before the week is out," said Penrose.

Marchbank glared at him. "Keep cheering me up why don't you?"

"I was only envisioning the worst case scenario."

"Well envision it somewhere else." In hope Marchbank turned to Colon, the retired police inspector and occasional wicket-keeper. "Have you any ideas, Phil?"

Colon stroked his not insignificant chin in thought, an affectation that he employed whenever his advice was being sought ever since he'd seen Basil Rathbone doing it when playing the part of Sherlock Holmes in *The Hound of the Baskervilles*. Rathbone's chin-stroking, however, had resulted in a much higher crime-solving success rate.

"Not at the moment I'm afraid," said Colon, then added as an afterthought, "I could always get the bugger locked up I suppose."

"Yes, but if you got him locked him up he wouldn't be able to play for us would he?" said Marchbank pragmatically.

"He wouldn't be able to play for Upper Medlock either."

"Well there is that I suppose."

"Might be worth putting on the back burner in case he does decide to play for them," mused Penrose.

"Yes well it's front burner ideas we want, preferably with the gas ring turned up full," said Marchbank.

"I think we might be well advised to take a leaf out of the Upper Medlock book and concentrate on what we can offer him for free," said Sturgess. "If you can't beat 'em join 'em."

"I don't see what I can give him for free," said Doyle-Davidson. "I'm a chartered surveyor; people aren't in the habit of having things surveyed every five minutes."

"Same goes for me," said Roderick. "People generally only want their accounts doing once a year."

"I could give him some free financial advice, maybe," said Sneed, after a moment.

"We're trying to get him to play for us, not ruin him," said Marchbank, recalling the financial advice Sneed had given him when he was changing his pension plan.

Sneed opened his mouth to offer yet another lame excuse for causing Marchbank to be £4000 out of pocket but closed it again without saying anything, probably judging that it was better to let sleeping dogs lie, or at least give them the chance to go back to sleep.

"I *suppose* I could give him free dental treatment," Penrose said grudgingly. "But I don't see why I should be the only one making with the freebies."

"I'd willingly bury him for nothing," said Sturgess, then added quickly, rather making a mockery of his generosity, "Nothing too fancy of course, I'm not prepared to run to more than pine. But I'm sure you all know the crippling price of wood nowadays."

"And I suppose I could conduct the funeral service at a reduced rate," said the Reverend Green.

"If he needs to be buried he'll hardly in a position to turn out for us, will he Reverend?" said Roderick.

Silence settled like a dark cloud on the gathering for several moments.

"Perhaps...?" said Marchbank eventually, a thoughtful look replacing the troubled one that had occupied his face since the meeting had begun.

"Yes?" said Penrose.

"Perhaps we're approaching it from the wrong angle?"

"What other angle is there to approach it from?" said Doyle-Davidson.

"Well....I was thinking that maybe instead of trying to come up with something that might encourage him to play for Lower Medlock we ought to be trying to think of something that will *discourage* him from playing for Upper Medlock. Or something that will ensure that he *can't* play for them. Preferably something that ensures he can play for us, if we can manage to talk him round."

"Such as?"

Marchbank shrugged in exasperation. "Well I don't

know, I'm just running things up the flagpole here in the hope that one of you will salute it. But surely there must be something we can do?" He took a drink of *The Dun Cow*'s house red in the hope it might aid his thinking. It had never managed to before, in fact the mellow Australian shiraz tended to dull the creative process if anything, but there was always a first time.

"He could have an accident I suppose?" said Roderick, after a minute's absence of flag saluting had slipped by. "Quite a few people go shooting in the woods behind The Olde Mill Cottage; I've bagged the occasional wood pigeon myself." He raised an enquiring eyebrow. "A stray bullet perhaps?"

"Christ we don't want to kill him," said Doyle-Davidson, alarmed.

"I wasn't suggesting we do. I meant just wing him."

"Wing him?"

"An arm or a leg or something. Enough to put him out of action."

Marchbank shook his head from side to side as though unable to believe his ears. "If we put him out of action he won't be able to play for us will he, you prick."

Roderick looked hurt. "It was only a suggestion; a work in progress."

"Yes well it's never going to progress far enough for him to be any use to us with a fucking bullet in him, is it?"

"Perhaps we could all have him for dinner?" said Doyle-Davidson brightly. "As a dinner guest, I mean," he added quickly, should any of his colleagues, particularly Roderick and Colon, think he meant they resort to cannibalism in order to solve the problem. "Perhaps we could each wine and dine him royally?"

"I've already thought of that," said Marchbank with a weary sigh. "He thanked me profusely, said he really appreciated the gesture but he likes to watch his waistline and limits himself to dining out no more than a couple of times a week, and that the next four weeks have been taken up by invitations from members of the Upper Medlock team."

Roderick grimaced. "That shower of shit have really gone to town on him, haven't they."

"Yes they bloody well have," said Marchbank. "So get your thinking caps on, the lot of you, and let's get something sorted out."

The group went silent for several minutes. Penrose suggested that more drinks might get their brain cells working more actively. Marchbank said that the Australian shiraz hadn't been much help and suggested a round of shorts, something that they could get down them quickly, as the sooner they got their brain cells up and running the better. A round of Courvoisier was ordered and consumed. But despite the stimulus of more alcohol and the donning of thinking caps it was beginning to look as though there would be nothing further forthcoming in the way of suggestions when Penrose suddenly said, "What was that you said about Blackbottom Brook disappearing under The Olde Mill Cottage, Jerry?"

"Just that," said Marchbank. "It disappears under the property and comes out the other side. Goes right under the middle of it apparently."

"And that's the reason it was decided that half the cottage is in Upper Medlock and the other half in Lower Medlock?"

"That's what I said, didn't I."

Penrose fell silent for a moment. "What if it didn't?"

"What?"

"What if it didn't disappear under the cottage and come up on the other side?"

"But it does," said Marchbank impatiently.

"*Now* it does. But what if it didn't? What if it was diverted?"

"Diverted ?"

"What if we diverted it; altered its course so that it went round the cottage on the Upper Medlock side? *Leaving the whole of The Olde Mill Cottage in Lower Medlock.*"

Marchbank looked as though all his birthdays had suddenly arrived at once. He beamed at Penrose and reached over the table to hug him. "If you weren't so bloody ugly Penners I'd give you a kiss."

"Is it possible? What Perce is suggesting?" said Roderick in a state of excitement, not quite able to believe a solution to the problem could be so simple.

"Of course it's possible," said Marchbank. "Christ Almighty man, people dug the Suez and Panama Canals, I'm sure they can dig a channel round The Olde Mill Cottage; Blackbottom Brook can't be more than four or five feet wide at the most."

"Digging on that scale doesn't come cheap," said Doyle-Davidson, donning his chartered surveyor's hat. "It would cost us a pretty penny."

"About how many pretty pennies?" said Marchbank.

"Difficult to say off hand. Quick estimate, ball park, say ten grand."

"That's less than a grand each if we split it equally amongst the team. A bargain at twice the price for a player of Jonny Pickering's calibre I'd say."

Roderick wasn't wholly convinced. "Perhaps we should

conduct a feasibility study?"

"Bollocks to any feasibility studies, we're doing it," said Marchbank. He turned to Doyle-Davidson. "Get me a price, Archie. And just as quick as you like."

CHAPTER EIGHT

Heavy Roller
1. A very heavy cylinder of metal used by the ground staff, to improve a wicket for bowling.
2. A very fat member of the Pentecostal Christian Church.

The forecast by Penrose that Scrivener might soon be re-thatching the roof would be realised, to Marchbank's chagrin, the following day, Scrivener having given the roof the once-over and finding part of it in need of refurbishment. What Marchbank wasn't aware of, and what would have poured more oil on his troubled waters, was that two more members of the Upper Medlock side, Jack Robinson and Justin Threlfall, would soon be making a start on Pickering's overgrown garden, which nature had taken a grip of during the time the cottage had stood empty, and which they had assured the grateful Pickering they would soon restore back to its former glory.

"We're not doing enough, lads," said Duckworth, when everyone had settled down.

"Well I don't see what else we can do," said Spragg.

It was Friday night in *The Grim Jogger* again. A week had passed since Spragg had revealed that Pickering had taken up residence in their village, or, has had since been revealed, maybe not in their village but possibly in the village of Lower Medlock. All the regulars were in attendance, with the addition of the aforementioned Threlfall and Robinson, but with the exception of Gibbon, who was travelling overnight to Cornwall so as to be first in the queue with his renovated Moorcroft vase and German helmet for the *Flog It!* valuation day in Truro that Saturday.

"Well I must admit I can't think of anything myself," said Duckworth, gloomily gazing into his pint of Old Stumpy as though the answer may be lurking in the bottom.

"Perhaps we're doing enough already?" said Spragg. "I mean we're doing a fair bit as it is."

Duckworth didn't share Spragg's optimism. "How many times do you want telling, Shane? He says he won't play for either side if it's going to cause any trouble."

"So why are we even talking about it then?"

"Because if we do enough for him it might make him change his mind," said Duckworth. He looked round the company. "Unless anybody has got any better ideas?" His team mates' vacant faces informed Duckworth that they hadn't. "So we need to be thinking up things we can do for him that we aren't already doing."

"Well there's nothing I can think of," said Robinson, when it looked as though no one else was going to say anything. "We're already doing everything for him but wipe his arse when he goes to the lavvy."

"Hiya lads, got held up," said another member of the team, Peter Potts, joining them.

"Potty. Just in time. We've got just the job for you," said Harris, to the amusement of everyone but Duckworth. "I wish you buggers would take this seriously," he complained.

"We are taking it seriously, Les," said Spragg. "But if

Pickering won't play for us he won't play for us. And as long as he doesn't play for Lower Medlock either I don't see what odds it makes."

"If he *does* play for them it'll make a lot of odds," said Duckworth. "And knowing that load of wankers they'll be trying just as hard as us to find a way to make sure he does. So we have to make sure he doesn't. And we can best do that by trying to come up with something we aren't giving him yet, some service we aren't providing him with that will make him prefer us to them."

"I should think a bloke like Jonny Pickering has got pretty much everything he needs already," said Harris. "I mean he can't be short of money if my two kids are anything to go by, they've never got a packet of Quigley's Quavers out of their hands."

"There *must* be something" said Duckworth in earnest, as unwilling to let it go as a dog with a bone.

"Perhaps somebody's missus can iron his shirts?" said Robinson. "I'm not married myself but most of you have got wives."

"I'm not married," said Spragg.

"You are," said Duckworth.

"I won't be if I try to get the wife to iron somebody else's shirts, I'll be dead."

"It's not a such bad idea though," said Duckworth thoughtfully. "I mean some people's wives are a bit sweeter-natured than your Michelle, Shane." Spragg didn't seem at all offended by Duckworth's opinion of his wife's disposition. Duckworth looked around the table and settled on Threlfall. "How about your missus, Jason?"

Threlfall scoffed. "You must be joking. I can't even get her to iron *my* shirts let alone somebody else's."

"Put me down for it," said Francis generously. "I'll put them in with mine, the wife won't know any difference, she's short-sighted."

"She must be if she married you," said Robinson.

Duckworth smiled despite himself. When the others had stopped laughing at Francis's expense he said, "I noticed cracks in the corners of a couple of his windows when I was cleaning them; are any of you any good at glazing?"

Threlfall, perhaps anxious to redeem himself after being unable to provide a suitable solution for the ironing of Pickering's shirts, volunteered immediately. "I can glaze windows; I can take care of that, no sweat."

"Good, good. Any other suggestions?"

"I can do a bit of dry-stone walling," said Potts, perhaps anxious to get rid of any potential bottom-wiping duties. "I could check the walls surrounding the cottage, see if they want any repair work doing on them."

"That's *better*, we're getting somewhere now," said Duckworth, cheering up a little. "Anything else?"

"I do all my own wallpapering," said Robinson. "If he wants any wallpapering doing I can do it."

"And I can do any re-wiring if there's any re-wiring wants doing," said Spragg.

"Jesus, look at the body on that!" said Bristow.

Duckworth turned angrily on his vice-captain and was about to wade into him for changing the subject yet again when he noticed that the lounge bar, seconds before alive with the hum of boozy conversation and the sounds of games of darts and dominoes, had gone suddenly quiet. Bristow was looking in the direction of the bar, his eyes almost out of their sockets and his mouth agape, joined now by the rest of the team and all the other male occupants of the room who had sight of the bar.

Tilly Turner, the object of their looks of lust, had just sallied into the bar, her latest boyfriend in tow. Tilly was, as the expression goes, drop dead gorgeous. As a schoolgirl, not all that long ago, her history teacher had privately thought of her as the girl who launched a thousand wanks, a fair proportion of which were his own.

A truly lovely blue-eyed long-legged blonde, Tilly was wearing a pair of denim shorts that were so brief she appeared to be wearing them from the inside. Her top was equally revealing, an unbuttoned red and white gingham shirt, the shirt ends knotted tightly together under her breasts, lifting and supporting them in the absence of a bra and displaying them to their best effect. Which was a quite wonderful effect. It was said in the villages that the sight of Tilly could give a man an erection at fifty paces. In an admission that it wasn't only *Beyoncé* he lusted after Franny Francis had claimed that this was a conservative estimate and that the distance at which she could cause a man to suddenly have a stiffy on his hands (and in Francis's case, soon afterwards, *in* his hands) was more like a hundred paces, as it had happened to him on a couple of occasions.

Robinson, ogling Tilly along with the others, was now struck with a eureka moment of the same magnitude as the one that had struck Penrose when the idea of diverting Brookbottom Brook had suddenly hit him.

"Tilly Turner!" he exclaimed jubilantly to Duckworth. "We can give him Tilly Turner."

CHAPTER NINE

The Dr Hodgkinson Affair

Back in 1968, if The Reverend Hartley had remained in the church clock tower until everyone had left the vicinity, *The Church Clock Affair* might have been attributed to an act of God. However he was spotted leaving the tower by one of the Upper Medlock team and in next to no time, the Medlock villages' grapevines being particularly fruitful, everyone knew it was an act not of God, but of The Reverend Hartley.

Shawcross, the Upper Medlock captain, complained bitterly and sought to claim the match by default. Wilks, the Lower Medlock captain, comfortably batted this demand aside with the excuse that the vicar must have had a brainstorm. Shawcross countered this by saying that in order to have a brainstorm one must first have a brain, an organ that The Reverend Hartley was clearly lacking: hadn't the man already proved that he was completely off his rocker by booking both a funeral and a marriage into the St Matthew's calendar for the same day just because he'd had an altercation with the groom over a game of bar skittles? Wilks claimed this was a one off. Shawcross said it was at least a two off because to his certain knowledge the vicar had done the same thing two months previously following a quarrel with a deceased man's wife.

Wilks had no alternative but to accept the vicar's culpability in the affair. He was not, however, prepared to hand victory to Upper Medlock, and suggested that the match be declared null and void. Shawcross accepted this offer but only on the understanding that The Reverend Hartley be banned from turning out for Lower Medlock in perpetuity. When the reverend was informed of the decision he replied that if he was not allowed to play then nobody else would be allowed to play either as he would make it his business to see that the church withdrew its permission for Lower Medlock to use the ground. After further negotiations between the two clubs it was agreed that The Reverend Hartley would be allowed to play but that any runs he scored would be ignored.

In the event the reverend had played his last game for Lower Medlock as on hearing about the incident his bishop, probably having realised that a man who had the sort of mind that could come up with such a devious idea was wasted on a small village like Lower Medlock, immediately promoted him to a more prestigious church within the diocese.

And so the fixture continued, although now with an ever-present undercurrent of distrust. Six years on this distrust, still simmering after *The Church Clock Affair*, boiled over.

September 2 1974.

Upper Medlock v Lower Medlock. Wickets pitched 2pm. Umpires J Rawlinson, T Meakin.

Lower Medlock 189 all out.

Upper Medlock

J Barnes b Shippon 12
A J Chester c and b Southfield 24
L Peebles c Francis b Cheyney 17
A Emley run out 15
T R Waters(C) b Shippon 11
L A L Smith b Breeze 13
F Clunes run out 0
E Peebles c Cheyney b Whittaker 2
A Jones b Whittaker 4
A Jennison not out 0
Dr V Hodgkinson not out 76
  Extras 16
   Total 190 for 9

Upper Medlock won by 1 wicket.

In what was turning out to be a very one-sided fixture Lower Medlock were seemingly coasting to an easy victory. With nine Upper Medlock wickets down, all the Lower Medlock bowlers in fine form, the team's catching and fielding leaving nothing to be desired, the home team had struggled to a score of 55. Then fate put in an appearance; a welcome appearance so far as Upper Medlock was concerned, not so welcome for Lower Medlock. For at that point Dr Hodgkinson, who had arrived at the crease at the fall of the wicket of Alastair Jones, faced his first ball from fast swing bowler Andy Whittaker, who was on a hat trick. Never having achieved this notable feat, and obviously eager to do so, Whittaker put everything he had into the ball. It was an excellent delivery. Dead on a length, fast, and swinging viciously from leg to off. It was just the sort of ball that Dr Hodgkinson didn't like.

In fact the doctor wasn't all that keen on any kind of ball. He was a batsman, to use the term loosely, who failed to trouble the scorer as often as not, whose method of batting was to wait until he saw the ball coming then close his eyes and take a wild swipe at it, having found from experience that he scored more runs this way than he did with his previous method of leaving his eyes open and trying to play it stoically with a straight bat. On average he connected with one in five of his uncultivated clouts. When he didn't connect it was followed, sooner or later, but usually sooner, by the sound of falling timber behind him. When he did connect the result was almost always a four, and occasionally, thrillingly, a six. However he didn't connect very often and his highest score, accumulated in a career spanning twenty three years, was a hundred and nine. Occasionally he connected with the ball with only a thick or thin edge of his bat and when that occurred anything could happen: if the ball kept low he might be caught by the wicketkeeper or in the slips, if it went high a fielder in the outfield might claim him as a victim, and on the occasions when the ball was neither caught nor fielded immediately he would scamper down the wicket for a run, maybe two if his luck was in. In the current match he caught the ball with a thick edge, whereupon it ballooned into the air, soaring high over leg slip, before coming to rest first bounce no more than a yard from the long leg boundary in the middle of a large, ripe, freshly shat cowpat. (Although the land was now a cricket pitch, as opposed to the field it had been until 1953, the cows in the adjoining field had not been informed of this, or if they had they had ignored it, and quite often wandered onto the pitch to do their business, or maybe just for an aimless stroll round or to chew the cud, as cows are apt to do.)

First on the scene was Alan Southfield, who had raced over from his position at third man, his eye on the ball every step of the way, intent on taking a spectacular catch and sealing a memorable victory for his team. Disappointment clouded his face as the ball fell to earth when he was still a couple of yards away. He was not, however, downhearted; he was downhearted when he saw it bounce off the ground and land in the cowpat. It had almost disappeared, only a small circle of red visible in the deep khaki of the cowpat, as though a very small cardinal was almost completely submerged in it.

It was immediately obvious to Southfield that extracting the ball from its faecal grave would be a far from straightforward task; at least it wouldn't be a straightforward task for him, a fastidious man who didn't even like to get his hands dirty let alone get them dirty by using them to pick up a cowpat-encrusted cricket ball. He paused to consider the matter, a hand under his chin in the archetypal manner of someone in deep thought.

"What's the matter?" Richard Breeze called out, trotting over from his position at deep square leg.

"The ball's landed in this cowpat," said Southfield, pointing at it.

"Well fish it out and throw it back."

Southfield considered this suggestion only very briefly before saying, a little shamefaced. "Would you mind doing it, Richard?"

Back on the pitch, Dr Hodgkinson, on arriving at the bowler's end, said to umpire Rawlinson, "I hope you're counting these, Umpire?"

"I most certainly am, Doctor," said Rawlinson, "That

makes you five."

In the meantime the captain, George Shippon, had trotted over to Southfield. "What's the holdup, Alan?" He glanced around, puzzled. "Where's the ball?"

With a nod Southfield indicated the cowpat. "You can just make out the top of it, see."

"Well get it out man, don't just stand there, they're still running," Shippon urged.

"Richard's going to get it out," said Southfield,

"I bloody well am not," said Breeze angrily. "Why should I get it out? You get it out; you were the nearest fielder to it."

Southfield shook his head. "Well actually I wasn't. I think you'll find that the man fielding at leg slip was nearer than I was."

"Eddie Priestley?" said Shippon. "Are you joking? You can't expect Eddie to chase after the ball, with his back, the poor man can barely walk let alone chase after a ball, that's why he fields at leg slip, because nobody ever hits it there and if he gets tired he can have a rest behind the stumper."

Southfield shrugged. "Well *I'm* not getting my hands covered in cow muck, and that much is for certain."

"And I most certainly am not," said Breeze.

Shippon had a brainwave. "We'll claim a 'dead ball'."

"Excellent idea," said Southfield, "Claim a dead ball, Skipper."

"Nip over to the square leg umpire and tell him then."

"It isn't dead, it's in a cowpat, if the information you have given me is correct," said umpire Meakin, after Southfield had reported the incident to him.

"It's as good as dead," said Southfield.

"Not good enough," said Meakin. "*Law 23, Dead ball.*

2. Ball finally settled.' The ball has to be finally settled."

"It can't be more finally settled than stuck in the middle of a bloody great cowpat," said Southfield, a little narked. "I would have thought it was very settled."

"Whether the ball is settled or not is a matter for the umpire to decide," said Meakin. "And I am of the opinion that it hasn't. Seventeen."

"What?"

"Seventeen."

"Seventeen what?"

"Runs."

"Runs?" said Southfield, bemused.

"I'm counting the runs Dr Hodgkinson is accumulating while you're stood here arguing the toss. Eighteen."

Southfield bit his tongue and before he was tempted to commit violence on the umpire hurried back to Shippon to report the bad news. In the meantime Ted Frankland had appeared on the scene from deep-mid wicket. "What's going on?"

Shippon quickly put him in the picture.

"Perhaps you can kick it out," he suggested after a moment's deliberation. "Sort of work the toe of your boot under it and hoof it out."

"Good thinking, Ted Frankland" said Shippon, and turned to Southfield. "Kick it out."

Southfield's eyes widened in horror. "What? You must be joking. I'm not putting my boots in there, they're brand new, I've only just bought them."

Shippon shot him a withering glare. "You won't pick it out, you won't kick it out, you can't instruct the umpire properly that it's a dead ball, just what the hell *can* you do?"

"Get out of the bloody way, I'll do it," said Frankland,

stepping forward before Southfield could think of a suitable reply.

"Well it *was* you who suggested it after all," said Southfield airily.

"You just shut it," said Shippon. "You've played your last game for Lower Medlock."

Southfield was aghast. "What? Just because I refuse to get cowshit on my brand new cricket boots?"

"For exactly that."

The ball proved to be more difficult to extract than Shippon had imagined and a good three minutes had passed before it popped out, during which time several kicks had demolished most of the cowpat, quite a bit of which landed on Southfield's whites, to his great displeasure.

"Now wipe the cowshit off it on the grass," urged Shippon, "and chuck it back."

"There might not be time for that, George," warned Breeze, flinging an arm in the direction of the still-scampering Dr Hodgkinson and Jennison. "God knows how many they've runs they've clocked up by now."

Whether God might have known or not is perhaps a question for believers and non-believers to debate; however Hodgkinson knew as he'd just checked with Umpire Rawlinson - sixty-six, leaving his side needing ten more runs for victory.

Had Shippon been aware of this he would have realised that there was ample time to convey the ball back to the pitch and break the wicket, thus running out either Hodgkinson or Jennison and therefore winning the match. He could have walked the ball back to the wicket, even at a leisurely pace, maybe stopping to commiserate with Eddie Priestley about his bad back on the way. But he didn't.

Instead, he picked up the still cowpat-soiled ball and threw it in as hard as he could. However in his hurry to get it back he threw it not to the wicketkeeper, whose gloves would have prevented his bare hands from coming into contact with the dung-coated missile, but to the bowler, Whittaker, whose hands of course didn't have the benefit of gloves.

Which was unfortunate, because if any member of the Lower Medlock side was more fastidious than Southfield, and thus not at all keen to get his hands soiled with cow dung, it was Whittaker. This being the case, when he saw the ball heading directly his way he chose not to catch it but to step to one side, with the idea of allowing it to drop to the ground, from where he would pick it up, albeit gingerly, and break the wicket. However he had failed to note that Umpire Rawlinson was standing directly behind him, and therefore in the path of the ball once he had stepped aside, with the result that the ball hit Rawlinson on the temple, whereupon he fell unconscious to the ground.

"Fuck me!" exclaimed Cheyney, who was standing nearby. He bent over and looked at the prostrate umpire. "I hope you haven't killed him, Whittaker."

"Me?" said an aggrieved Whittaker. "It wasn't me who threw the ball." He looked around. "Anyway where *is* the ball?"

Cheyney couldn't see the ball either. "He must have fallen on it," he concluded. "He must be lying on it."

"I'll roll him over," said Whittaker, and bent down to do just that.

At that moment Hodgkinson, completing his sixty-eighth run, came skidding to a halt beside them. "I'm a doctor!" he cried melodramatically.

Whittaker looked up. "Yes I know you're a doctor,

Doctor. It's Andy Whittaker, I saw you about my waterworks last week."

On his dash down the pitch whilst notching up his sixty-sixth run Hodgkinson had had an excellent view of the incident and had come to the same conclusion as Cheyney as to the whereabouts of the ball. "Don't move him," he ordered.

"What?" said Whittaker.

"The umpire," said Hodgkinson, and continued in his stern doctor voice. "On no account must he be moved."

"But he's lying on the ball," protested Cheyney.

Hodgkinson was unmoved. "He could swallow his tongue."

"But he's lying on the fucking ball."

The addition of an expletive to Cheyney's plea made not a scrap of difference to the doctor's opinion. "You don't want him asphyxiating himself, do you?" he said. "Surely you don't want to be responsible for the poor man's death?"

"Well....no. But...."

"Then leave him as he lies and call for an ambulance at once," said Hodgkinson, and with that set off back down the pitch for another run.

"Hey where are you going?" shouted Whittaker after him. To glory, said Hodgkinson to himself, and wasted no breath on a reply. The doctor, although keen as mustard, only just scraped into the Upper Medlock side when other players were on holiday or otherwise indisposed; this could well be the only chance he would ever have of making a name for himself on the cricket field and it was not a chance he was about to turn down.

Two minutes later Umpire Rawlinson called out, "That makes you seventy-six now, Dr Hodgkinson."

Hodgkinson stopped running, beamed, and he and Jennison walked triumphantly side by side back to the pavilion, to be welcomed into the open arms of their overjoyed team mates.

CHAPTER TEN

Draw Stumps
1. Declare the game over; a reference to (with)drawing the stumps from the ground by the umpire.
2. What a dentist does.

Tilly Turner, clutching her ankle, a look of pain creasing her pretty face, hobbled up The Olde Mill Cottage drive - if Jonny Pickering happened to be looking out of the window the last thing she wanted was for him to see her walking normally, not when she was about to tell him she feared she had sprained her ankle and could he possibly offer assistance? She imagined that her cry for help would be all it would take to achieve her object; it certainly would with all the other men she'd come across in her short but very full life.

As Tilly eased her way slowly to the front door she imagined herself seated on one of Pickering's easy chairs, a chintz one very probably she imagined, country cottages always seemed to have chintzy furniture. In her mind's eye she was leaning back, her long blonde hair cascading around her shoulders, an arm shielding her eyes as if fearing the worst, as Pickering ministered to her. The famous cricketer himself was on his knees, the better to examine her ankle and, even better, where he could get a good look up the very short skirt she had carefully chosen for the occasion. If, by some miracle, once he'd had an eyeful of the sexual heaven to be found there, it hadn't led to them heading for the bedroom as though there were no tomorrow, she would tell him she thought she might have strained her thigh too, and could he please massage it, rub it better? If that were to happen they wouldn't even get as far as the bedroom, of that she was sure, they'd be at it right there and then on the living room carpet. She hoped he had a sheepskin rug, she liked having sex on a sheepskin; it seemed to bring the out animal in her, maybe because she was being made love to on an animal.

She reached the front door and glanced down at her perfectly-tanned breasts, unfettered as usual by a bra, struggling to break free from her skimpy white top like two bald-headed escapologists. She undid another button, composed herself, took a deep breath to pump up her breasts and rang the bell.

Although Tilly Turner's only income was money given to her by men, she had never for one moment seen herself as a prostitute. Indeed, if anyone had accused her of being a prostitute, or even suggested it, they would at the very least have got a slap on the face for their pains. Tilly did not have clients, she had boyfriends. Lots of boyfriends. They came initially from the two Medlock villages but, once she had exhausted the supply of local suitors (and in the process exhausted most of the suitors), supplemented by men from the half dozen nearby villages and the town of Middleham. Young boyfriends, old boyfriends, married boyfriends, single boyfriends, fat boyfriends, thin boyfriends, fit boyfriends, invalid boyfriends, Tilly took on all comers. (She had once had sex with a man in a wheelchair, a liaison that had been one hundred per cent satisfactory for both of them - once he'd remembered to put the brake on - and had even accommodated a man with a Zimmer frame, stood up in a bus shelter whilst he was waiting for his bus. The man and the bus came at the same time.) However she only ever dated one man at a time and never for more than a day or two. The only thing she demanded of her boyfriends was that they were well-heeled, or at least heeled well enough to be in a position to buy her a nice present, or give her money to buy one.

There was never a shortage of boyfriends. Before embarking on her chosen career she was sure there wouldn't be. By the age of thirteen she had already noticed the way men looked at her, and that the older she got the more they looked. So it was no surprise to her when, three years previously, having left school at the age of sixteen and taken a job as a barmaid at *The Shorn Sheep*, that all the male customers looked at her in a way they didn't look at the landlord, nor the way they regarded his not unattractive wife for that matter. The difference now was that in addition to looking at her the men often made suggestive remarks to her, and about her, within her hearing, usually couched in a light-hearted manner and cloaked in *double entendres*, but no less serious in its intent for all that. Therefore it came as no surprise, certainly not to Tilly, that in a matter of weeks she decided that perhaps a more agreeable way of making a living would be to stop hand-pumping the clientele's pints of bitter in favour of hand-pumping their sexual organs, along with the rest of the business that inevitably followed.

So all that the Upper Medlock cricketers had had to do, once they had decided that the gift of Tilly was absolutely the best thing they could do to help persuade Jonny Pickering to join their ranks, was to mention to her that the famous cricketer had come to live in The Olde Mill Cottage, and that not only was he very well set up but had a reputation for being the most generous of men. Any doubts that the idea might not appeal to Tilly were dispelled completely when Duckworth showed her a photograph of Pickering and she realised immediately that his handsome face was the same face that had been smiling at her from her daily packet of Quigley's Quavers for the last six years. It was an assignation made in heaven.

The front door of The Olde Mill Cottage swung open smoothly and silently on hinges newly-oiled by the member of the Upper Medlock team who had been deputed to do all the odd jobs that needed doing around the cottage. Two minutes later, having tearfully explained her problem, Tilly was seated on one of Jonny Pickering's easy chairs and Pickering himself was on his knees in front of her, just as she had imagined, except that the chair was antique leather, not chintz, and the famous cricketer was much more handsome in the flesh than the picture of him on the packets of Quigley's Quavers, despite his having two black eyes. In fact she wasn't sure that the black eyes didn't make him look even more attractive, sort of all cuddly like a panda.

"Let's take a good look at it then." Pickering smiled reassuringly as he reached out to take her ankle in his hands. "See if you've done any permanent damage."

"There's nothing wrong with it," said Tilly, deftly swinging her leg to one side and putting Plan B into action.

About halfway through the two minutes she had spent in Pickering's company she had decided to dispense with Plan A. On setting eyes on her quarry she had taken a real shine to him and didn't want to take even the slightest chance of not finishing up in his bed, which might just possibly be the case had she stuck to her original plan. Who knew? He might be such a gentleman - and those men who played cricket for Upper Medlock had assured her that not only was he a gentleman but a gentleman who was by no means short of a bob or two - that he wouldn't wish to make love to someone who was injured, no matter how slight the injury, for fear of making it worse. (Should Pickering's black eyes have put Tilly off Duckworth had explained to her that he had received them whilst protecting the honour of a lady, which despite her way of making a living she had found ever so romantic.)

"Nothing wrong with it?" said Pickering, confused.

Tilly looked apologetic. "Please don't be angry with me. It....it's just that I wanted to meet you *ever* so much."

Pickering smiled. "You should simply have rung my doorbell."

"I didn't want to be a bother."

"You wouldn't have been, I assure you. Believe me, I'm used to it by now; I've already had three of the villager's ringing my bell this morning." He explained. "They wanted my autograph."

"I want your cock."

Five minutes later she was getting it, in Pickering's big double bed. Ten minutes later, when it was over and they were lying side by side, Pickering said, "Tell me, Tilly, are you always so....direct?"

Tilly shrugged. "If you're turned on by somebody why mess about?"

Pickering smiled. "Why indeed?" Under normal circumstances he would have been surprised at his words; he was a man who never slept with a girl on the same day they met. However Tilly was, as they say, something else, a girl that any man who still had a pulse would be far from likely to turn down.

"Did you enjoy it?" Tilly turned to face him as she said this. "I did."

"Very much so, Tilly."

Tilly smiled a coy smile. "I know you did." After a moment she said, "Do you want to do it again?" I mean after the commercial, she thought, but said, "In a bit, like. No rush."

When Duckworth and company had approached Tilly they had been adamant that during the time she was with Pickering she should try to get him to play for their cricket team. Even though she had promised she would she had remained undecided about it - a promise to a man had never counted for much in Tilly's world ever since she had discovered that most of *their* promises were just so many words. Besides, how would they know whether she had asked Pickering to play for them or she hadn't? However she had really enjoyed herself and was certain that there would be a nice present heading her way, so why not?

"They tell me you're a cricketer," she said artfully.

"I used to play a bit, yes."

She pushed him playfully in the ribs with her elbow and smiled. "Don't be so modest. You must be dead famous to get your picture on packets of Quigley's Quavers."

Pickering shrugged. "Well quite famous, I suppose."

"And much better looking, even with two black eyes, than that footballer whose picture is on potato crisp packets, what's-is-name, him with the ears?"

"Why thank you."

Tilly was silent for a second or so then suddenly said, "Wait a minute! Oh my God!" Then, as though the idea had come to her completely out of the blue, "Why don't you play for *my* team?"

"What?"

"Why don't you play for Upper Medlock? Oh please say you will, Jonny; I'm their biggest fan."

"Really?"

"I'll say; I watch them every week, home and away, rain or shine, good times and bad, never miss. It would be just great if you could play for us."

Pickering gave a rueful shake of his head. "I'm not so sure that I can do that, Tilly."

"Oh *please*, Jonny." Tilly sat up abruptly in bed and clasped her hands together in a gesture of prayer. "*Please*! It would mean ever so much to me. Please say you'll play for Upper Medlock, even if it's only just the game against those stuck-up snotgobbling arseholes from Lower Medlock," she said, innocently bringing to mind the expression Duckworth had used in describing the enemy, at the time he put the proposition to her.

On hearing Tilly's words Pickering raised an eyebrow and for the first time began to feel that perhaps there was something about the situation that was not quite right. One of the men doing The Olde Mill Cottage's garden and the man who was at that very moment thatching its roof had used exactly the same words when describing the Lower Medlock team.

"Oh *please*, Jonny?" Tilly implored him again. By way of an incentive she pushed the duvet to one side, took his penis in her hand and stroked it, a promise of what would inevitably follow if he went along with her request.

Despite his suspicions Pickering was unwilling to turn Tilly down flat as he quite fancied another session of the fabulous sex he'd had just minutes before, so he said, "Well, Tilly, I shall have to think about that."

Tilly leaned over, gave the end of his rapidly swelling penis a big kiss, licked it a couple of times for good luck and said, "Oh thank you, Jonny. Thank you, thank you, thank you."

Pickering held up a stern finger of warning. "I'm not promising anything mind."

Tilly, feeling his penis now completely hard in her hand, said, "I am, a lot, so let's fuck," and without further ado cocked her leg over him and sat astride him. "And then you can buy me a nice present."

Pickering looked sharply at her. "What?"

"Then you can buy me a nice present." She noticed his less than pleased look. "What's the matter? All my boyfriends buy me presents. Or give me some money to buy myself a present, which is the same thing."

Pickering gave the resigned sigh of someone who realises he has been taken for a sucker. "So you're a prostitute then."

"What?"

If Pickering had been looking at Tilly when she said this, had seen the anger in her eyes, he might have kept his mouth shut. But he didn't. "You're a prostitute," he said again.

He engaged eye contact with her just in time to see her fist heading for his nose, but not in enough time to take avoiding action before it smashed into it with a sickening thud and the sound of breaking bone and crushing sinew.

CHAPTER ELEVEN

The Yorkshire Ringer Affair

Before the 1950s the village of Medlock depended almost exclusively for its living on the large wool manufacturing mill which either directly or indirectly employed over half of the inhabitants, villagers whose daily needs were served by the shopkeepers, tradesmen and professional people who comprised the rest of the population. By 1965, after finally losing the battle with cheaper foreign imports it was never going to win, just one of many such battles fought by similar wool and cotton mills in the 60s and 70s, the factory had closed down.

Still standing to this day, now the home to a dozen or so small manufacturing units, the four storey brick building is situated in what is now Upper Medlock. At the time of the closure all the better houses, detached or superior semi-detached properties, the homes of the village's businessmen, doctors, solicitors, master tradesmen etc, were in what is now Lower Medlock. Most of the dwellings in Upper Medlock were two-up two-down terraced houses, built by the owners of the wool factory to house their workers.

Things are very much the same to this day except that Lower Medlock has become something of a dormitory town, its ranks swelled by an influx of professional people wishing to have the benefits of living in the country whilst making their living in the city, its up-market housing stock swelled by new properties built to accommodate them. In contrast Upper Medlock is predominately home to the people who work in one or other of the small businesses housed in the old wool mill or behind the counters of the villages' shops, or are small businessmen on their own account, carpet cleaners, painters & decorators and, as we have already learned, window-cleaners and milkmen. Because of this, and assuming that the terms Upper Class and Lower Class were still in vogue, the village of Upper Medlock would definitely be lower class whilst the village of Lower Medlock would just as definitely be upper class. 'Upper Class' people being of the nature they are, the villagers of Lower Medlock have always maintained that it is the lower class people of Upper Medlock whose village should have been named Lower Medlock whilst their own village should have been named Upper Medlock. It is an incongruity that has always stuck in their collective craw, especially in the craws of the members of the Lower Medlock cricket team, and is the reason that in 1983 their current captain and leading light, Grant Fairfax, took even greater satisfaction from what became known as *The Yorkshire Ringer Affair* than he might otherwise have done. Because there was no one, but no one, of a lower class than the Yorkshire Ringer.

September 6, 1983.

Upper Medlock v Lower Medlock. Wickets pitched 2pm. Umpires J Statham, M Wilks.

Upper Medlock

J Fearon lbw b Bashforth 0
D Thickett (C) b Bashforth 0
A A Weeks retired hurt 0
P Greaves hit wicket b Bashforth 0
L Bracegirdle b Bashforth 0
M Moran b Bashforth 0
J B L Moran b Bashforth 0
R Pickering lbw b Bashforth 0
J R Collins retired hurt 0
W Edale did not bat
L Tweedie did not bat
  Extras 12
    Total 12l

Lower Medlock 13 for 0.

G Fairfax (C) not out 9
J Penberthy not out 4

Lower Medlock won by 10 wickets.

The Lower Medlock side had been having an exceptionally bad time of it in the late seventies and early eighties. Not only had they not beaten Upper Medlock during the previous five years but in four of the games they had been soundly thrashed, and would more than likely have been thrashed in the fifth had not Fairfax called it off at the last moment on the pretence that eight of the Lower Medlock team had suddenly gone down with African Sleeping Sickness, a disease inconveniently brought back from Nairobi by their slow right arm bowler Johnny Leach, along with his duty frees and examples of African art, following a sales trip to Kenya. The reason for Upper Medlock's supremacy was simply that their current eleven was markedly stronger than usual at the self same time that the Lower Medlock side was a good deal weaker than in previous line-ups, so in 1983, faced with either the pain of another sound thrashing or having to come up with another unlikely excuse for the fixture to be called off, Fairfax gathered all the members of the team together with the object of trying to find a way out of the dilemma.

"Well you can forget telling them I've got African bloody Sleeping Sickness for a start," said Leach with some feeling, after Fairfax had opened the meeting and explained the position. "People believed it. No one would come within a hundred yards of my house for weeks."

"I doubt they'd fall for that one twice, Johnny," said Fairfax, without a trace of sympathy.

"They won't get the bloody chance," said Leach. "We had no milk deliveries for a month, no newspapers, no post, no nothing. 'You'll have to get some milk from the shop', Miriam said. 'And while you're at it get some lamb chops from the butchers; he hasn't delivered again either'. Leach scowled. "You want to try getting into Spar and the butchers when they think you've got African Sleeping Sickness, by Christ do you, they bolt the door and man the barricades when they see you heading their way. The bloke at the bakers threatened me with a shotgun."

"All right, all right, Johnny," said Fairfax, in an attempt to pacify the disgruntled Leach.

"What we need is the Upper Medlock lot to have African Sleeping Sickness," chimed in Penberthy. "Especially that fast bowler of theirs, what's he called, Tweedie. That would slow the bastard down a bit."

With memories of the only time he had ever faced a ball from the Upper Medlock fast bowler another member of the team, Simister, said ruefully, "He needs to be slowed down, that one. My bollocks will testify to that."

"You should always wear a box," said Fairfax.

"I *was* wearing a bloody box. It might as well have been an egg box for all the protection it gave me."

"What we need is a ringer," said the side's off-spinner, Sargent, knowledgeably.

Sargent could usually be counted on to speak good sense but on this occasion his suggestion made little sense to Fairfax. "A wringer?" he said, crinkling his brow. "What are you proposing, Sarge? That we trap Tweedie's dick between the rollers?"

"Not a wringer," said Sargent patiently. "A *ringer*. A player of an altogether different class who has been entered into a competition dishonestly. Except in our case it wouldn't be dishonest; we can play anyone we wish, there's nothing in the rules to stop us."

"Well it's an idea," said Fairfax, seeing a little light at the end of what up until then had been a long, dark tunnel. "But where would we get such a man?"

"Yorkshire," said Sargent, immediately and with great certainty. "That sort of underhanded jiggery-pokery goes on all the time in the Yorkshire leagues; it's rife, they're devious bastards Yorkshiremen, they're known for it."

Fairfax didn't look any further for an answer and the following weekend he and Sargent gave their away fixture against Compton-cum-Netherwood a miss in favour of travelling to Yorkshire in search of a ringer. On the Saturday enquiries were made in Settle, Harrogate and Greasebrough.

On the Sunday contact was made with the ringer whom the vast majority of those questioned had recommended, one Freddie Bashforth. A suitable arrangement with Bashforth was quickly agreed to whereby for a fee of thirty pounds plus five pounds for every wicket taken, plus expenses, the Yorkshireman would play for Lower Medlock in the match against Upper Medlock three weeks hence.

It had been observed by one of the men in Settle from whom Fairfax and Sargent had sought advice, and confirmed by all the other men of Settle, Harrogate and Greasebrough who had been canvassed, that if Freddie Bashforth had had his head screwed on properly not only could he have played for Yorkshire but for England too, and in all probability to great effect. Named after the great Freddie Trueman by his cricket-mad father, Bashforth, a six feet four inches tall beetle-browed man with a permanent scowl was an impressive sight, his shoulder-length black hair with its central parting giving him the appearance of a particularly nasty pantomime villain peering maliciously through the curtains.

Bashforth was as fast a bowler as Trueman and twice as uncouth, which, as anyone who has ever crossed the path of Fearless Fred will know, is a long way from being couth; a bowler who, not satisfied with merely bowling a batsman out, helped him on his way back to the pavilion by fixing him with a manic glare and saying "Now fuck off out of it before you get hurt!" (Conveniently forgetting that most of them had already been hurt.) He was allowed to get away with this as a degree of uncouthness is looked upon as an asset in certain parts of Yorkshire, rather than the disadvantage it is seen as in other counties.

Unfortunately, however, while Bashforth's bowling was of lightning pace his temper was even quicker, a defect in his personality that caused him to live his life more often in trouble than out of it and in gaol almost as often. Currently banned from playing anywhere in Yorkshire, for his many misdemeanours, which included braining an umpire with one of the bowler's end stumps when the official had turned down a dubious leg before wicket appeal, and had then made matters worse by telling him that the next time he turned down an appeal he'd ram the stump up his arse pointed end first, Bashforth played most of his cricket in Lancashire, in Cheshire, in Staffordshire and in disguise, especially when playing in Yorkshire, which he still did on occasion despite being banned.

On the day of the match none of the Upper Medlock team expressed surprise on seeing amongst the Lower Medlock ranks someone they had never seen before - occasionally new people moved into the villages, occasionally they liked a game of cricket and found their way into the side. However, although not expressing surprise, they did express a great deal of trepidation. This was conveyed in various observations, one of which was "I don't fancy our chances against him!" another "Bloody big isn't he!" a third "Nasty-looking bugger isn't he!" and, by Bracegirdle, one of the more loquacious members of the Upper Medlock team, "I don't fancy our chances against that bloody big, nasty-looking bugger!"

They were wise to be wary of Lower Medlock's new player. They would have been even wiser had they forgotten all about the match and gone home; to forget the match altogether and spend the afternoon sitting on the railway lines playing with razor blades would have been preferable.

Although named after the great Freddie Trueman the former England test bowler was not Bashforth's bowling hero. That honour fell to another England bowler from another era, and another county, Nottinghamshire. His name was Harold Larwood, the man who in the 1930s initiated what came to be known as 'bodyline' bowling, a technique in which the object was not to try to make the ball hit the wickets but hit the batsman, preferably on the head, where it would do the most damage. This manner of bowling appealed enormously to Bashforth's base instincts and he always included a generous measure of it in his bowling spells. (Larwood was only known to Bashforth courtesy of grainy black and white newsreel clips of the 1932-33 series against the Australians in which the legendary English fast bowler had broken the hated opposition both in body, literally, and soul. Bashforth had studied the footage minutely in order to learn Larwood's technique - and often just for the pleasure of seeing batsmen battered into submission - and had learned well from his scholarship.)

The fears of the Upper Medlock team were realised no later than the very first delivery of the match, a Yorker that Bashforth, keeping his bodyline bowling attack on hold for a couple of balls, sent down at ninety miles-per-hour, and which removed not only Fearon's middle wicket but, before the ball had reached the wickets, most of the toecap of his right boot, breaking two of his toes in the process.

Once Fearon had been helped in tears from the field of play and umpires Statham and Wilks had decided, after a short consultation, that the batsman had been out leg before wicket rather than bowled, since the ball had hit his toe a split second before hitting the wickets, the match, and the carnage, continued.

Bashforth, even against batsmen of county standard, was a force to be reckoned with. Against the village cricketers of Upper Medlock he was a lethal weapon. In the entire innings he bowled a total of eighteen balls. None of them were hit. Three of the batsmen were; the aforementioned Fearon; Weeks, who ducked and narrowly avoided the first ball he received and, expecting a similar ball from Bashforth's next delivery ducked and received a direct hit on his Adam's apple when it came through at bouncer height; and Collins, perhaps shell-shocked after observing what had happened to Fearon and Weeks, who stood transfixed and glassy-eyed in the crease, allowing Bashforth's sharply rising just short of a length delivery to crack him a fearful blow on the elbow, fracturing his funny bone. The remainder of the team who batted used their bats to defend themselves with rather than in any attempt to score runs. None of them connected with the ball, which either bowled them or went for a four, the sheer pace of the ball beating the wicketkeeper, even though he was almost standing on the boundary ropes.

The numbers ten and eleven in the side, Edale and Tweedie, undoubtedly influenced by the fate of those teammates who had been forced to retire hurt, two of whom in the meantime had been despatched to the local cottage hospital, did not bat, despite impassioned entreaties from their captain, Thickett. When his pleas fell on deaf ears Thickett threatened them that if they didn't stop behaving like bloody wimps and get out there and bat that as long as he was captain they would never play for Upper Medlock ever again. To which Tweedie replied that that would be perfectly all right with him as he didn't want to play cricket ever again if it meant facing mad bastards like Bashforth.

The match, which started at two-o-clock, was all over by three. Apart from the fate that had befallen the three batsmen who had retired hurt there was one other casualty and one very close call. The casualty occurred when Peter Greaves, on returning home at 3.15 rather than the more usual seven or eight-o-clock in the evening, discovered his wife in bed with the local chimney sweep. (It transpired that the affair had been going on for three seasons; Greaves had had no idea, his wife being fastidious to a fault in laundering the bedding, this being paramount as she liked the chimney sweep to service her in his work clothes.) The very close call came when Fairfax, working on the principle that Bashforth hadn't dismissed those batsmen who had retired hurt and had refused to bat, attempted to pay him £30 plus £30 for the six wickets he had taken, rather than the £30 plus £50 that Bashforth had contracted for. However he quickly changed his mind when Bashforth informed him that if he didn't cough up and fucking quick about it he would flatten him twice, first with his fists and then with the heavy roller.

The year following the *Yorkshire Ringer Affair*, if the amount of boasting by the Lower Medlock side about the outcome of their next annual fixture had not made it abundantly clear to the Upper Medlock side that Freddie Bashforth would be turning out for them again, their captain Grant Fairfax made absolutely sure they knew by telling them. If he had kept the information to himself and just got on with it the Lower Medlock side would almost certainly have chalked up as emphatic a victory as they had on their previous encounter. However, thanks to Fairfax's need to crow about it, the Upper Medlock side, after allowing him the pleasure of doing so, promptly pulled the mat from under him and his team by refusing point blank to fulfil the fixture if the Yorkshireman took any part in the proceedings. Their argument, understandably, was that it was unfair to bring in an outsider, especially someone who was a far superior cricketer; in fact it was little short of cheating. Lower Medlock countered this by saying that there was nothing to stop Upper Medlock bringing in a similar outsider of their own. Upper Medlock met this with the argument that if both sides were to bring in ringers either one side's ringer would cancel out the other's, or it would become a contest as to which side could come up with the best ringer instead of a contest about which of the two villages was superior at the game cricket, and in either case it would be better to do without ringers and save themselves some money. The Lower Medlock side eventually saw the sense in this and an agreement was struck that in future only men born in the villages, or those who were currently domiciled in the villages, would be allowed to take part in the match.

CHAPTER TWELVE

Dead Ball
1. The state of play in between deliveries, in which batsmen may not score runs or be given out.
2. A testicle that can no longer produce sperm.

Archibald Doyle-Davidson replaced the phone and smiled the sort of smile that said all was well with the world. The call had been from O'Casey & Nephews, the contractors entrusted with the job of diverting the course of Brookbottom Brook. O'Casey himself had informed him that the job was finished, two days beyond the agreed completion date, but still in good time. The Olde Mill Cottage was now firmly and absolutely in Lower Medlock, thus rendering Jonny Pickering unable to play for Upper Medlock even if he had wished to. Job done and dusted. And, best of all for Doyle-Davidson, he had trousered a couple of thousand pounds for himself out of it.

The chartered surveyor had been reasonably accurate in his estimate of the cost of the work. Following the meeting in *The Dun Cow* he had wasted no time in asking the civil engineering contractors Wilde & Son for a quotation. They had come up with a figure of £8750. Doyle-Davidson got

Marchbank to OK the quote and set about collecting £730 from each member of the team. He had since accomplished this, not entirely painlessly, even though they could all well afford it. He then contacted O'Casey & Nephews, a contractor who he knew from past experience would be cheaper than any other contractors he had dealings with, but who could still be relied on to do an acceptable job provided you kept a close eye on him. In the event, due to pressure of work, Doyle-Davidson hadn't been able to keep as close an eye on him as he would have liked. However it didn't seem to have made any noticeable difference, O'Casey & Nephews had delivered.

For a few moments Doyle-Davidson bathed in the satisfaction of a job well done and the even bigger satisfaction of two thousand additional pounds nestling in his bank account. Sufficiently refreshed, for there is nothing better than an increase in a man's finances to improve his disposition, he picked up the phone again and dialled Marchbank's number. He took his time in imparting the good news to the Lower Medlock captain, with particular emphasis on his own vital part in it, and arranged to pick him up at his office, from where they would proceed to The Olde Mill Cottage to view the work.

"I thought Wilde & Son was doing the job?" said Marchbank an hour later, on alighting from Doyle-Davidson's Mercedes 500S and seeing two large yellow trench diggers with 'O'Casey & Nephews' emblazoned on them in foot-high bold black lettering.

"They let me down," said Doyle-Davidson smoothly, the lie slipping effortlessly off his tongue. "Wanted to put the date back, didn't they. Well I wasn't having any of that of course." He cocked an enquiring eyebrow at Marchbank.

"Didn't I mention it?" Without giving Marchbank the time to deny it he went on. "Anyway I brought O'Casey & Nephews in; I've used them before on numerous occasions, they're very reliable, a touch dearer than Wilde & Son, but I'll make up the difference myself." He spread his hands magnanimously, the great philanthropist. "Well it's the least I can do; after all it was I who obtained the quotation from Wilde's in the first place."

This information was taken in by Marchbank with a very large pinch of salt. If Doyle-Davidson wasn't making something out of it himself Marchbank would be the next Pope, and he wasn't even a catholic. However it was of little import. The only thing that mattered was to make absolutely sure that Jonny Pickering would never be able to play for Upper Medlock, at least not unless he upped sticks and moved there, and there wasn't very much likelihood of him doing that as he'd only just moved into his present home. This objective had been achieved. They could now move on to the next stage and get to work persuading him to play for Lower Medlock.

Whilst they had been talking O'Casey, a small, skinny, crumpled-looking individual not too much unlike a man-sized leprechaun, the similarity enhanced by his emerald green overalls and ruddy-cheeked complexion, jumped off one of the trenchers and breezed up to them. Marchbank thought he recognised him as one of the two Irishman who a few years previously had re-tarmaced his drive and gone over the tortoise that had lived happily in his front garden for years, but as he wasn't absolutely sure - he never took much notice of the appearance of tradespeople - he chose not to challenge him on this. O'Casey doffed an imaginary hat, gave a curt little bow and smiled. Marchbank half-expected him to say

'Top of the morning to you' but instead he grinned and said politely, "Good day to you, gentlemen."

"And a good day to you, O'Casey," said Doyle-Davidson warmly. He indicated Marchbank. "This is my associate, Mr Marchbank."

"Top of the morning to you, Mr Marchbank," said O'Casey. His eyes narrowed as he peered at Marchbank. "Haven't I seen you somewhere before, sir?" However before Marchbank could say 'Yes, you're one of the blind buggers who tarmaced over my little daughter's tortoise' O'Casey continued. "You'll be wanting to inspect the quality of the workmanship?"

"That's the general idea," said Doyle-Davidson.

"Well you'll find everything very much in order, so you will. That feller Thomas Telford couldn't have done a better job in twice the time at three times the price, even if I say so myself." The contractor swept an inviting arm in the direction of his handiwork. "This way, gentlemen."

"Lead on O'Casey, lead on," said Doyle-Davidson.

O'Casey led them the few yards to where the brook had previously disappeared under the cottage. He puffed out his chest. "There she is."

"What the....!" said Marchbank, no sooner had his eyes lit on the scene.

"Oh so you've noticed already," said O'Casey with a smile. His Irish eyes twinkled. "There's not much chance of putting one across you is there, Mr Marchbank?"

"What's the matter, Jerry?" said Doyle-Davidson, having previously had eyes only for the new brook wending its pretty way round the front of The Olde Mill Cottage.

"What's the matter?" said Marchbank, his usual florid face an even deeper shade of red, his blood pressure having instantly shot up several notches. "What's the matter? I'll tell you what's the fucking matter. He's dug two fucking brooks, that's what's the matter!"

"What!" Doyle-Davidson took a look. Incredibly, Marchbank was right. At the same spot the new brook started its journey round the front of the cottage another brook of similar width commenced its journey round the back. He turned on the Irishman. "What the hell is going on here, O'Casey?"

O'Casey shrugged off what he obviously saw as a minor deviation to the script. "It was what you might call in the way of an unfortunate accident, so it was. You see to get the job done even before time - which I knew you would like very much, Mr Doyle-Davidson, sir, from my past dealings with your good self - I put two of my trenchers on the job instead of the one. I had one of my nephews set off digging where the brook comes up at the south of the cottage, and the other nephew setting off from here, where it disappears to the north of the cottage, the idea being that they'd meet in the middle. Unfortunately, however, the nephew heading north took the wrong route, as you might say. Well as you can see. I believe Sean must have had the plans upside down, easily done, a mistake anyone can make. That's why the job was a couple of days overdue. However the good news is that you've got two brooks for the price of one. Because I don't intend to charge you any extra."

By now absolutely livid Marchbank turned to Doyle-Davidson. "You are not to pay this bog-trotting Irish bastard a single penny until he's filled in that other fucking brook."

Doyle-Davidson hedged. "Er...."

"What's the matter?"

"Well I'm afraid...."The chartered surveyor wrung his

hands together as though a genie might suddenly emerge with a puff of smoke and haul him out of the mire he'd managed to drop himself into.

"You're afraid what?"

"That he's already been paid. It was part of the deal you see, cash up front."

"You twat!" Having voiced his opinion of Doyle-Davidson Marchbank wasted no further time on him and turned his attention to O'Casey. "The brook you've dug round the back of the cottage. Fill it in."

"You won't be wanting it then?" There was much surprise in O'Casey's voice. "I'll bet the man who owns the cottage wants it; there can't be too many residences that have a brook at the front *and* one at the back as well."

"Well there's going to be one less. So fill the other one in!"

O'Casey accepted this with a puzzled nod. "Well you're the boss. So there's just the question of the price."

"Price? What price?"

"For filling it in."

Marchbank gasped at the sheer effrontery of the Irishman. "You....you surely don't expect us to pay you for filling it in? For fuck's sake man, we didn't want you to make it in the first place."

"You see I've already got rid of the diggings we excavated, so there'd be the cost of trucking them back. Even if I could get them back, which I very much doubt, because they've probably been sold by now, the way things are in the trade," said O'Casey, Marchbank's objections having easily passed him by. "So I'd probably have to buy new. Then there's the labour of course. But, apart from that, I mean even if I had the doings and the labour I wouldn't be able to make a start on the job until next month."

Marchbank was horrified. "Next month?"

"At the earliest. O'Casey & Nephews is a busy firm, so it is. I think it's the reliability people go for. So if you wanted it doing any sooner you'd have to be after getting somebody else to do it." He looked thoughtful for a moment and said helpfully, "I believe Wilde & Son aren't too busy at the moment."

*

Later that evening, having spent the last four days and nights in the nearby picturesque coastal village of Snettering-on-Sea, Jonny Pickering returned to The Olde Mill Cottage. Although he had spent a most pleasant time whilst away - the estuary of the River Medlock teemed with wildlife and the river itself was alive with a variety of fish, and he had drunk his fill of both - in truth he would have rather remained at the cottage. However there was so much going on there that life had become if not intolerable, then much less agreeable than he had envisaged life in a country retreat might be: Spragg, having finished whitewashing the exterior of the cottage had then insisted on re-painting the walls of the interior in coloured emulsions of Pickering's choice; Robinson and Threlfall were still hard at work in the garden and making far too much noise about it; Piggy Higginbottom, the man detailed to do any odd jobs, was still finding plenty of odd jobs to do; and Scrivener was still at work re-thatching a large section of the roof.

It wasn't just all the work that was going on that Pickering found difficult to live with - that would end sooner or later, and his being absent from the cottage for a while and therefore unable to accept any further offers of free goods and services could only help in this regard - but there was also the almost constant stream of autograph hunters and well-wishers to his front door that he had to contend with, every one of whom, having obtained his autograph or wishing him well, implored him to play cricket for either Upper Medlock or Lower Medlock.

On the short journey home from the coast Pickering reflected on the events that had transpired since he had taken up residence at the cottage little more than a week ago. Not for the first time he began to doubt his choice of area in which to retire and got to wondering if some of the other places he had considered, the Lake District, the Cotswolds, Snowdonia, might have been a wiser choice. All right, he would probably have got wetter in Wales, but would he now have two black eyes and a broken nose? Unlikely.

One thing was certain; he wouldn't now be carrying the disfiguring injuries he was if he hadn't been the famous Jonny Pickering and the local cricket teams, in particular the Upper Medlock team, hadn't been trying everything in their power to get him to play for them. He was aware, too, that through his reluctance to say no he had to some extent invited the situation.

After much soul-searching he decided that the way forward was to tell both cricket teams that it would be unfair to play for either of them. He would convey this decision to them as soon as he got back, possibly before someone from the Upper Medlock team turned up on his doorstep to sweep his chimney, and ahead of the Lower Medlock team coming up with ideas for free goods and services they could shower on him, which he expected anytime soon. He shuddered to think what the Lower Medlock team, with their obvious greater spending power, might come up with in the way of sexual treats; probably a three-in-a-bed with Madonna and

Rihanna.

It would be difficult telling them of his decision, and he didn't yet know exactly how he would go about it without causing them offence, but he would cross that bridge when he came to it.

One bridge that he didn't cross when he came to it, as there wasn't a bridge there to be crossed, was a bridge spanning the new brook which had appeared in front of The Olde Mill Cottage since he'd last been there. It was dusk when he arrived home, but even if it had been broad daylight he might still have driven his car into it as drivers of cars are not generally looking out for brooks that might suddenly have appeared in front of their cottage whilst they've been away for a few days.

Fortunately he was travelling at no more than five-miles-per-hour when the front wheels of his BMW roadster left what had previously been the short driveway leading to the garage, and ended up in a watery grave. Although he received a severe jolt as the wheels hit the bottom of the brook, he didn't receive any injuries thanks to the air bags kicking in. However the luxury of air bags kicking in was not available when he climbed out of the car to investigate and fell into the brook. Which was regrettable enough in itself, but not nearly so regrettable as when he clambered blindly out of the brook, slipped on its muddy banks and knocked out his two front teeth on one of a pile of large stones that O'Casey had excavated and planned to pick up later for a wall he was building.

CHAPTER THIRTEEN

The Space Cakes Affair

Following *The Yorkshire Ringer Affair* the rivalry between the cricket teams of Upper and Lower Medlock heightened considerably.

But it was not just the relations between the cricketers that deteriorated; as a direct result of the bad blood between the teams relations between the villages themselves worsened. The annual cricket match, which had been conceived as a way of bringing the villages together in friendly combat, was now doing precisely the opposite. The animosity shown to each other by the residents, whilst not yet as intense as that displayed by the cricketers, was catching up fast: examples of the villagers of Lower Medlock referring to their opposite numbers as brain dead wankers and the villagers of Upper Medlock calling their adversaries toffee-nosed twats were by no means uncommon.

The incident attributed to spreading the hate from the cricket teams in particular to the villages in general occurred in 1985 when Upper Medlock resident Joe Scattergood and his wife Milly bought their fourteen-year-old daughter Phoebe a pony for her birthday.

The Scattergoods weren't wealthy people - Joe was a farm labourer, Milly had a part time job at *The Cakehole* cake shop - and although both of them would have dearly loved to buy Phoebe a much longed-for pony it was way beyond their means. However fate stepped in when Scattergood, on bemoaning his inability to satisfy his daughter's birthday wish one Saturday evening at the bar of *The Grim Jogger*, was approached by a stranger: the outside had overheard Scattergood's tale of woe, he might be able to help, he just happened to have a pony for sale and it was going for a very good price as he and his family were emigrating to Canada in a few days time, he was desperate to find a good home for it, he could bring it round to Scattergood's house the following evening when Scattergood could give it the onceover, no obligations, and if he liked what he saw he was sure they would be able to come to an agreement.

The following day the man turned up as promised with a fine pony which he soon sold to a delighted Joe for two hundred pounds. A few days later, on the occasion of Phoebe's birthday, Joe and Milly gave her the pony. Two days later an irate Henry Foster - who was at the time, incidentally and unfortunately, the vice-captain of the Lower Medlock cricket team - was on Scattergood's doorstep demanding to know what the hell his daughter Phoebe was doing riding about as large as life on *his* daughter Jessica's pony.

"Your daughter's pony?" said the baffled Scattergood. "But it's my daughter's pony; I paid two hundred pounds for it only last Sunday."

Foster was apoplectic. "Two hundred pounds? Two hundred bloody pounds? I paid three thousand pounds for that pony not six months ago, it's a thoroughbred; it was stolen from the field where Jessica keeps it, *also last week!*"

Foster not only had proof of ownership in the shape of a receipt from the dealer from whom he had bought the pony but also a photo of his daughter Jessica astride it. Reluctantly Scattergood handed over the pony.

That might have been that but Foster, not content with getting the pony back, couldn't resist telling Scattergood, in full view of whoever happened to be passing at the time, and at the top of his voice, that he had far better things to do with his Sunday mornings than track down horse thieves, and that he would be doing them if it wasn't for brain dead twats like Scattergood who believed there was nothing dodgy about the sale of a three thousand pounds thoroughbred pony for two hundred pounds. Still not content, over the next week Foster proceeded to tell everyone in Lower Medlock he could collar what had happened, and that it was all that could be expected from the lowlife that lived in Upper Medlock. His words seeped through to some of the villagers of Upper Medlock, who had previously never seen themselves as lowlife, and was spread by them to the rest of the village. Naturally everyone took offence and consequently relations between the villages started to go downhill.

They went even farther downhill and gathered pace two weeks later on the occasion of the Upper and Lower Medlock Operatic and Dramatic Society's (UALMOADS) annual coach trip to Scarborough. As usual the coach left to arrive in good time for the party to take in the matinee performance of the current Ayckbourn farce playing at the town's Stephen Joseph Theatre, a pleasure they had taken many times before and never tired of. As usual the rest of the day was free for the trippers to do as they pleased, and as usual the trip's organiser Betty Bates warned everyone to be back at the coach by seven-o-clock at the latest for the journey home. Come seven-o-clock, and after doing a head count, Ms Bates instructed the coach driver to leave. The coach had travelled barely a mile when it was pointed out that two of the ladies, Hannah Rowbottom and her close friend Polly Harkness, sisters-in-law from Lower Medlock, weren't on the coach, along with the obvious observation that they would have to return to Scarborough for them. It was not, however, obvious to Betty Bates, who wouldn't hear of it, and despite protestations from many of the trippers instructed the coach driver to carry on regardless.

Fifteen years previously when the UALMOADS had performed *Oklahoma*, and eight years later, when they had again staged that musical, Betty Bates, one of the society's founder members and leading lights, had played the plum role of Ado Annie. Last year, when they had again put on Rodgers and Hammerstein's perennial favourite, she had fully expected to be once more playing the part she had come to regard as her own. However the responsibility of casting the role fell to the show's director, Hannah Rowbottom, who, to the surprise of everyone, gave the part to her sister-in-law Polly Harkness's daughter Margery, who had recently joined the company. Whether or not this had any bearing on Betty Bates's decision to leave Hannah Rowbottom and Polly Harkness behind is a moot point; however most of the villagers, possibly influenced by the stolen pony incident a few weeks previously, believed it to be anything but moot, and much more likely to be a stone cold certainty.

Relations between the villages, already uneasy by this time, worsened. Women all but ceased to do their shopping in the shops of the other village; if they couldn't buy the goods they required in their own village they would have them delivered by a trader from one of the other nearby villages, or go without them, rather than break their embargo. The women of Lower Medlock chose to travel to Middleham to have their hair dressed, or relied on the services of a mobile hairdresser rather than have their hair cut, blown and set by *Hair Today*, the villages' only hairdresser; the women of Upper Medlock scorned Lower Medlock's *Browned off Sun Parlour* and either travelled the six miles to the village of Nettleton to top up their tan or remained unfashionably pale.

It was not restricted to the adults. Since the 1962 boundary change the former Medlock Junior School, now situated in Lower Medlock, had been school to the children of both villages: then they mixed quite happily, but now the children of Upper Medlock always sat next to children from Upper Medlock, children from Lower Medlock always sat next to children from Lower Medlock, and at playtime the children of each of the villages played separately; only when it came to fighting did they have anything to do with each other and then they had plenty to do with each other.

The revulsion of the residents of one village for their opposite numbers didn't spread to their pets, but now any villager of Lower Medlock who was in the market for a dog would be far more likely to buy a pit bull terrier, where previously they might have chosen a Labrador, in the hope that it would bite a resident of Upper Medlock. And vice versa.

Even so, nowhere was the hatred more in evidence than in the annual cricket match. In the matches in their respective leagues the average attendance was one man and his dog (more often than not a pit bull terrier). When they took the field against each other the attendance was getting on for eighty per cent of the combined population of the villages, close on three and a half thousand men, women and children. There had yet to be a pitched battle but wise people knew it was only a matter of time.

There had been fights galore; fights between rival factions in the crowd, fights between spectators and cricketers, fights between the cricketers of Upper Medlock and Lower Medlock, and, on more than one occasion, fights between members of the same team when it had been felt by one player that another player wasn't doing his utmost in the battle to defeat the odious opposition.

Sledging, even more so than in the bitterest conflicts between England and Australia, was a regular feature, employed liberally both by the players of either side and by the spectators, but especially the latter. A fielder had only to position himself within twenty yards of the boundary to be showered with abuse (and quite often also showered with manure from a nearby farmer's field). A ball that had been hoisted in the air by a batsman could not come down in the vicinity of a fielder without someone in the crowd shouting 'Drop it you cocksucking cunt', or worse. If the fielder did happen to drop the catch, which was likely to happen more often than not as concentrating on catching the ball with your back to a mob of spectators, any of whom might lob a half-brick at you at any moment, the very least he could expect in the way of abuse was a shout of 'Give him a bucket' and suggestions that a visit to the local opticians might not be a bad idea.

Ball tampering, the action in which a fielder illegally alters the condition of the ball to the benefit of the bowler, was rife. Picking at the stitching of the main seam or 'lifting' the quarter seam in an effort to aid swing is illegal; nevertheless it is practised in all levels of cricket from village match to test match, usually facilitated with the aid of a nail or beer bottle top or other sharp implement carried secretly in the trousers pocket and surreptitiously used when the umpires and batsmen aren't looking. Likewise, to polish the ball with illegal substances is against the laws of cricket but universally practised. It is normally only the players who consort to such illegal tactics but in the matches between the Medlock villages the spectators not only played a part but very often outshone the cricketers. Whereas the players, when polishing the ball, confined themselves to the tried and tested substances of hair gel, Vaseline, sugar, and lip balm, the spectators painted from a larger palette. Perhaps the most blatant way of bringing a brilliant shine to the ball was the utilization of a battery-powered floor polisher and buffer by the owner of the *Upper Medlock Do-it-Yourself Emporium.* This shenanigan was at least matched by the Lower Medlock spectator who made the most of a Black and Decker power tool's screwdriver attachment to lift the quarter seam of the ball, and the sander to leave its stitching in tatters.

The only time the respective villages' inhabitants weren't at each other's throats was in the provision of teas for the annual cricket match. Not even the feud between the villages was allowed to interfere with this.

The battle to provide the finest teas was long standing, almost as old as the battle for supremacy on the cricket field. Although the ladies had always prided themselves on their sandwiches and sausage rolls, without ever thinking much about it beyond hoping the victuals they provided were at least the equal to the catering of their opposite numbers, it wasn't until 1970 that the teas catering became a contest every bit as fierce as that on the cricket field, when Florence Jameson of Lower Medlock, fresh from a two week holiday in

Provence, upped the ante by putting on a most splendid frogs' legs quiche, and was overheard by one of the Upper Medlock ladies to mutter to a companion "Let them pick the bones out of that". Naive Avril Rogers of Upper Medlock suggested that Florence Jameson had probably meant the bones that required picking out of the quiche were in the frogs' legs, and for this reason she herself was going to avoid it. However the rest of the Upper Medlock ladies had no doubts what Mrs Jameson meant.

Twelve months later, when Upper Medlock's top cook Myrtle Henderson replied with a platter of wild pacific salmon goujons with a beluga caviar dip, the battle was fully enjoined.

In the years that followed the cricketers of both teams were provided with food fit for a king. It wasn't only at the match between the two villages that the ladies provided outstanding fare; during the season various recipes were tried out in the quest to provide the finest of spreads for the end-of-season encounter, and with such success that at least three men who previously had little interest in cricket joined the teams just for the food. The year after Upper Medlock's wild pacific salmon dish the ladies of Lower Medlock roasted a suckling pig. The following year the Upper Medlock ladies replied with quail stuffed in a partridge stuffed in a grouse stuffed in a pheasant stuffed in a duck stuffed in a goose stuffed in a turkey, and it was only because the Middleham branch of Waitrose couldn't supply them with a swan that the stuffing of birds with birds concluded with the turkey.

However, and despite dishes that wouldn't have been out of place at the most sumptuous of banquets, the foodstuff that was universally accepted to be the best, joyfully by the ladies of Lower Medlock, grudgingly by the ladies of

Upper Medlock, was Monica Mourne's chocolate brownies. The brownies, made to a recipe more secret and closely guarded than Colonel Sanders' Kentucky Fried Chicken recipe, and almost certainly better, were quite simply to die for: and for this reason were responsible for making the feud between the villages take on Hatfield versus McCoy proportions.

The teams had been enjoying Monica Mourne's chocolate brownies since she had been persuaded to bake them by Rose Timperley, the wife of the current Lower Medlock captain, in response to an absolutely mouth-watering Eton Mess put on by the Upper Medlock ladies the year before. "It will take nothing less than your brownies, Monica. The ladies of Lower Medlock are depending on you," said Rose. It was all that was needed for Mrs Mourne to don her pretty pinny, roll up her sleeves and get baking.

By coincidence, ever since the introduction of the brownies, Upper Medlock, at the time a stronger outfit than their adversaries, had won the annual match. One night in *The Grim Jogger*, with the fixture just a week away, a few members of the team were bewailing their recent record when one of them jokingly said that maybe the reason they were losing was because Monica Mourne's chocolate brownies had put a jinx on them.

The statement had received a forced laugh from almost all the others, any other sort of laugh far from their lips with another defeat in prospect, but after a moment the only one who hadn't laughed, Dave Leishman, said mysteriously, "We could *get* them to put a jinx on Upper Medlock."

"What do you mean?" said Gordon Procter.

"Space cakes," said Leishman.

"Space cakes? What are those?" said Monica Mourne's

husband, Mike.

"Chocolate brownies laced with cannabis. If the Upper Medlock lot were to get a couple of space cakes down their throats during the tea interval they'd be good for nothing. They wouldn't know whether they were appearing in a cricket match or *The Lord of the Rings meets King Kong on Ice*."

"Drugs?" said Leonard Butterworth, one of the more innocent members of the team. "You're surely not suggesting we should drug the opposition?"

"Can you think of a better way to give us an edge?" said Proctor, warming to the idea by the moment.

"And the beauty of it is," said Leishman, his eyes now lighting up at the prospect, "The beauty is that it won't make any difference if they're batting or bowling after they've had the space cakes, they'll still make one almighty balls if it."

In the event it was the Lower Medlock team who batted first. Whether there would have been a different outcome had they bowled first no one will ever know, but the result would have been the same.

September 8 1989.

Upper Medlock v Lower Medlock. Wickets pitched 2pm. Umpires J Roberts, B Driscoll.

Lower Medlock, 210 all out

Upper Medlock

B Berkeley not out 0
S Lambert not out 0
  Extras 0

Total 0
Match abandoned. (Very)

The addition of cannabis - easily acquired from one of the Lower Medlock players who was partial to the occasional spliff himself - to Monica Mourne's chocolate brownies, thus transforming them from a confectionary into a deadly weapon, was accomplished without too much trouble by Mike Mourne. There was of course no way in the world that Mrs Mourne would have countenanced the addition of any other ingredient, let alone cannabis, to her famous brownies. There was a slight hitch when returning to the kitchen earlier than expected from the hall - where Mike had told Monica she was wanted on the telephone - she discovered her husband mixing her bowl of brownies mixture, but he managed to forestall any suspicions she might have been harbouring by playing the sycophant and telling her it was something he did behind her back at every opportunity as the brownies were so delicious he liked to lick the spoon. And there was a further concern when, on removing the brownies from the oven, Monica remarked that they hadn't risen quite as much as they usually did and she was going to throw them away and bake a fresh batch. However Mike managed to assure her that her eyes must be playing tricks on her and that the brownies were quite perfect.

On the day of the match the brownies took their usual pride of place at the very centre of the food laden tables. Monica Mourne had made the usual quantity, four dozen, which meant that during the tea interval at the close of the Lower Medlock innings there were more than enough for several of the Upper Medlock team to consume more than the customary two each (the Lower Medlock team members having been warned to steer well clear of them of course).

Mike Mourne hadn't quite finished the job to his satisfaction before he had been disturbed by his wife whilst mixing in the cannabis resin to the brownie mix, so it was by no means certain that the drug was evenly distributed in the finished article. What is quite certain is that Benjamin Berkeley, the Upper Medlock opening batsman, had consumed three of the space cakes, at least one of which must have contained more than its fair share of cannabis if his performance with the bat was to be believed. The Upper Medlock vice-captain only received one ball - although in addition to the usual red one he saw heading his way at what appeared to be in the region of two hundred miles-per-hour, there was also a blue one, a green one, and a yellow one with purple spots - all of which he comfortably managed to miss when he attempted to hook any of them to the square leg boundary. If he had managed to hold on to his bat when his impetus caused him to spin two complete circles before losing his footing and falling flat on his face he might have survived for another ball, but it slipped from his grasp, flew ten yards behind him, whereupon the bottom edge of it hit the Lower Medlock wicketkeeper plumb between the eyes. "Run," shouted Saul Lambert, Upper Medlock's other opening batsman, on observing that the ball had dropped out of the pole-axed wicketkeeper's hands to the ground, and that there was little danger of him retrieving it in the immediate future. Hearing the call, Berkeley hauled himself off the ground and started running - but not to the other wickets but in exactly the opposite direction, towards the sightscreen, pausing only to pick up his bat from beside the prostrate wicketkeeper. Observing this, Lambert, himself suffering from the effects of two space cakes, became even more bewildered than he already was and stopped in his tracks halfway down the wicket. Steven Haynes, fielding in the gully and thus quite near to the ball, quickly ran over, picked up the ball and threw down the batsman's wicket.

"How is he?" appealed Haynes, turning to the square leg umpire. He might as well have appealed to the sightscreen. Umpire Driscoll didn't know how he was; whether he was out, not out, or even what day it was. Umpires feasted from the same tables as the players and Driscoll, particularly partial to chocolate brownies, had eaten four of them. On their walk out to the wicket prior to the commencement of the Upper Medlock innings Umpire Roberts, who hadn't had a chocolate brownie as sweet things always gave him toothache, had been surprised when Umpire Driscoll had remarked what a wonderful orange sky it was and didn't the church tower look nicer now they'd painted it turquoise and put that pink giraffe on top, but had put it down to Driscoll being something of an eccentric. (Driscoll had once umpired a match dressed in an astrakhan coat, Russian fur hat and wellington boots. He explained airily, when asked about his attire, that he had felt like a change.) Now, instead of standing at square leg in order to give decisions on stumping and run out appeals, he was as prostrate on the ground as the wicketkeeper, and, despite not having been hit between the eyes by a cricket bat, just as unconscious.

An appeal for a doctor to attend the comatose pair was made. Dr Chambers, the Upper Medlock left arm spin bowler, answered the call at once. Chambers, who had had two of the brownies, went first to Driscoll, felt his pulse, laughed like a maniac and pronounced him dead. Having completed his diagnosis he made his way to the wicketkeeper and did exactly the same except that he laughed louder and continued to laugh all the way back to the pavilion.

At that point Umpire Roberts took it upon himself to abandon the game as a draw.

Two of the Upper Medlock team had been on space cake trips before and suspected that they were now on another, so it didn't take them long to finger Monica Mourne's chocolate brownies as the cause of the outrage. Naturally the Lower Medlock team denied all knowledge but the Upper Medlock team knew the truth of the matter, once they had all recovered.

CHAPTER FOURTEEN

Bouncer
1. A fast short pitched delivery that rises up near the batsman's head.
2. What Dolly Parton has two of.

"What's that you said?" said Duckworth, cupping a hand to his ear and squinting down at Scrivener from the top of his ladder.

"Two Blackbottom Brooks," Scrivener replied, a bit louder.

Duckworth's face creased in a puzzled frown. "*Two* Blackbottom Brooks?"

"I figured you'd want to know."

"I'll come down." Duckworth dropped his wash leather into the bucket hooked to his ladder and returned to *terra firma* from the bathroom window he had been cleaning. "So what's all this about two brooks then?"

"Like I said. I went to Jonny's cottage this morning to finish off the thatching and these two brooks have suddenly sprung up. One goes round the front of the cottage and the other goes round the back."

Duckworth shook his head, mystified. Fond of fishing

himself and aware that Blackbottom Brook had some nice brown trout in it he could see where a man might like a brook flowing past the front of his house instead of underneath it. But one at the back as well?

"I wonder what he wants with two brooks?"

"Search me."

"I don't suppose you thought to ask him?"

"He's not there to ask. There's no sign of him. His car isn't there either."

"I wonder where he's got to?"

"Search me. Anyway I didn't think too much about it at first; if a man wants two brooks that's his business as far as I'm concerned. But I'd just got up on the roof to make a start when Marchbank turned up."

"Marchbank ?" Duckworth's head jolted back on his shoulders as if on a coiled spring at the mention of the enemy. "Why didn't you tell me?"

"I'm telling you now."

"Is he still there?"

"Search me."

Duckworth's eyes narrowed. "I wonder what the hell he wants?"

"Search me."

Duckworth shook his head hopelessly. "I do keep searching you, Tommy; but not in the hope that I'll find out very much."

"I knew about the two new Blackbottom Brooks, didn't I?" said Scrivener, a bit miffed. "And Marchbank taking more than a bit of interest in them."

"Sorry. Sorry, Tommy." Duckworth patted Scrivener on the back; it wasn't his fault. "It's all this worry about getting Jonny to play for us and not playing for Lower

Medlock."

*

Duckworth would have been even more worried had he known that Jonny Pickering, during his visit to the local cottage hospital after falling into the brook - his second visit that week following his visit a few days earlier to have his broken nose re-set - had had second thoughts about declining to play for either team and had decided to play for Lower Medlock. On reflection, and even though he could see that it may well cause some ill-feeling, he considered it was no less than the Upper Medlock team deserved. It was, after all, their fault and nobody else's that he now had two black eyes; all right, it might have been the Lower Medlock captain who had given him one of the black eyes, but that was accidental, it was Upper Medlock's Duckworth who had been responsible for the fracas. And it was most certainly the Upper Medlock cricket team who were the cause of his broken nose, courtesy of their champion Tilly Turner, whom they had obviously put up to it. He wasn't at all convinced they didn't have something to do with landing him in hospital a third time either; he had no way of knowing who had created a brook in front of The Olde Mill Cottage whilst he had been away, but someone had, and if forced for an opinion would have put money on it being the men who had rarely been out of his sight since he had taken up residence. So the way he saw it, taking everything into consideration, his turning out for Lower Medlock against Upper Medlock would be precisely what they warranted and would serve to teach them a lesson.

The large stone on which Pickering had knocked out his two front teeth on clambering out of the brook hadn't been the only stone to trouble him that night. The other one was the large stone on which he'd banged his head when falling into the brook. Feeling distinctly groggy, and left with blurred vision from the effects of being on the losing end of the argument with both stones, he had phoned for an ambulance on his mobile phone. By the time it arrived his head had cleared. Rather than bother the paramedics further he thought to apologise to them for calling them out unnecessarily before sending them on their way. The paramedics, however, insisted they would be failing in their duty if they didn't check him out. Having given him the once over they feared a possible concussion and were adamant that he would have to go to hospital for expert opinion. After examining him the night nurse, Nurse Scrivener, confirmed the paramedics' diagnosis and insisted he stay overnight with a view to a doctor examining him the following morning.

Whilst he was waiting Pickering seriously considered paying to stay on privately at the hospital, regardless of what the doctor might diagnose. The way he was feeling a few days convalescence would be just what the doctor ordered, even if the doctor didn't order it. It was comfortable and peaceful at the hospital, but more than that, it was safe from people who gave him black eyes and broken noses and who were more than likely responsible for his now being minus his two front teeth; and, whilst there could be no guarantee, the chances were that as long as he remained in the sanctuary of the hospital he wouldn't be subjected to another assault on his person. However no sooner had he had the idea than Nurse Scrivener, in a conversation designed to cheer him up, happened to mention that she was married to one of the Upper Medlock's cricket team. This being the case, and remembering the last time he had been in close proximity to a female with connections to the Upper Medlock team, he had abandoned the idea before she could get round to trying to persuade him to play for them and he ended up with another injury.

*

Duckworth, with Scrivener in tow, wasted no time in getting to The Olde Mill Cottage to find out exactly what was going on there. What was going on left him even more puzzled: two of Wilde & Son's labourers were filling in the newly-created brook on the Lower Medlock side of the property.

Following the discovery of O'Casey & Nephews' botched job Marchbank had called an emergency meeting at *The Dun Cow*. It had been decided, by a majority of eight to two - the two being Colon, who was still in favour of getting Pickering locked up and O'Casey & Nephews with him, and Penrose, who still had designs on winging him with a shotgun - that there was nothing else for it but to get the additional brook filled in with all possible speed and at all costs, or at least the lowest costs they could get the job done for. Doyle-Davidson said that O'Casey & Nephews would probably fill in the new brook for the lowest cost and Marchbank said he would fill in Doyle-Davidson, at no cost at all, if he ever mentioned the name of that fucking Irishman in his presence again. It was proposed and agreed unanimously that Wilde & Son should be asked to do the job.

The following day Marchbank, who had put himself forward as the best man to take on the responsibility of seeing the operation through, got in touch with the contractors. As luck would have it they had spare capacity, thanks to a hold-up due to a snag with the planning permission required for a job they had been due to start that morning. Marchbank, who in his capacity of Deputy Chairman of the Lower Medlock Parish Council had caused the snag, wasn't at all surprised. Wilde & Son agreed to fill in the brook for a price of £1000, plus materials of approximately £2000, ballpark. Marchbank said this seemed a bit steep, and remarked wittily that he didn't want to buy a ballpark he just wanted a brook filled in. Wilde and Son told him he could either like it or lump it. Marchbank liked it. It was arranged that a start would be made the following morning at nine-o-clock sharp. At eight forty-five sharp Marchbank arrived at The Olde Mill Cottage, perhaps fearful that Wilde & Son might do an O'Casey & Nephews and fill in both the new brooks.

The first thing Duckworth saw when he and Scrivener arrived at the cottage was one of Wilde & Son's labourers shovelling builder's rubble into one of the brooks. Another labourer was loading more rubble into a wheelbarrow from a flat bed truck. Duckworth turned to Scrivener in surprise. "You didn't say anything about anybody filling in one of the new brooks?"

"I didn't know anything about it," said Scrivener, just as surprised as Duckworth. "It wasn't being filled in when I left."

"I wonder why they're filling it in?"

"Search me."

Duckworth made his way over to the labourer on the truck.

"What's going on, mate?"

Before the man could answer Marchbank's voice rang out from the cab. "He is carrying out my orders. *If it's anything to do with you!*"

Although he had felt the necessity to oversee the job Marchbank didn't see why it couldn't be done from the comparative comfort of the truck. Initially he thought he might call on Jonny Pickering and perhaps mention, should Pickering have noticed that two new brooks had suddenly appeared and that no sooner had they appeared than one of them was being filled in, and was perhaps wondering why, that it was due to a ghastly error by the local Clerk to the Council, whose balls he would have on a shovel at the next meeting of the parish council. However Marchbank had noticed Scrivener on the roof, and Scrivener might have wanted to know the same thing, so had thought better of it. It was apparent though that he wouldn't be able to avoid Duckworth's questions so easily, judging from the attitude struck by his opposite number when he appeared red-faced at the open window of the lorry's cab.

"What's going on here then?"

"None of your business," said Marchbank, and made to lower the window.

Duckworth put his large window-cleaner's hand on the top edge of the window, stopping him. "If it's anything to do with Jonny Pickering it is my business," he said, thrusting his head forward challengingly. "Seeing as how he'll be playing for Upper Medlock against your lot."

Marchbank laughed. "In a pig's eye he will."

"Oh yes? And why is that?"

"Because he won't be able to play for Upper Medlock once the brook has been filled in, that's why." Even as the words were leaving Marchbank's mouth he regretted saying them. The less Duckworth knew about what was going on at The Olde Mill Cottage the less he would be able to do anything about it. Not that he *would* be able to do much about it, but even so it would have been better if Duckworth had been kept in the dark, discretion being the better part of valour. He consoled himself by acknowledging that valour had had less than a starring role in his life thus far, and that he'd managed pretty well without it, and waited to field

Duckworth's next question.

It wasn't long in coming.

"What are you talking about?" he said, keeping a firm hold on the top of the window in case Marchbank should try to close it again.

"You will find out in the fullness of time," said Marchbank airily. "Anyway I've wasted enough of my time explaining things I don't have to explain to the likes of you."

With that Marchbank turned away from Duckworth and re-focused his beady-eyed attention on the man filling in the brook, in the hope that it would make him work faster.

"It's like it's on an island, isn't it," said Scrivener, joining Duckworth.

"What?" He frowned impatiently. "What are you going on about now?"

"The cottage. It's like it's on an island. Well for the time being it is; it won't when they've filled the new brooks in."

Duckworth still couldn't make any sense as to what was going on. "Why go to the trouble of having a new brook made at the front and back of the cottage and no sooner than you've done it have them filled in?"

"Search me."

"What are you doing for the rest of the morning?" said Duckworth, after dwelling on the mystery for a moment further and getting nowhere. "And don't say search me."

"I was going to finish the thatching off."

"Leave that. Give me a hand to get in touch with the rest of the lads. This calls for an urgent meeting."

*

Had Jonny Pickering been at home when Wilde & Son started filling in one of the new brooks it would have saved him having more pain inflicted on his body than it had already suffered. On leaving hospital, however, he had other things to take care of before returning to The Olde Mill Cottage.

After delivering Pickering to the cottage hospital earlier that morning the paramedics, following standard procedure, had reported the accident to the police. After viewing the scene the police had arranged for the damaged car to be towed out of the brook by Woodside Auto, the Middleham garage they always called in to deal with vehicles damaged in traffic accidents (an arrangement which, incidentally, made them a nice little earner). They then proceeded to the cottage hospital to question Pickering about the incident. Pickering had said he could tell them very little about it, and would they kindly find out who was responsible for digging a brook in front of his house, and having found them get them to fill it in because he didn't want a brook there. The police said they would do what they could and would report back in due course if they had anything to report but that they didn't hold out much hope in cases like this.

Pickering's first stop on leaving the cottage hospital was at the Lower Medlock dental practice of P. Penrose to check out the damage to his teeth and determine what could be done about it.

It was, of course, as Penrose immediately realised when Pickering presented himself, an opportunity to offer his services for free, in the way that many of the Upper Medlock players had done and were still doing, and thus go some way to redressing the balance. To give Penrose his due he made determined efforts to do this, but in the end couldn't quite bring himself to do it. Try as he might he couldn't get it out of his head that the goods and services provided by the Upper Medlock side were as nothing compared to the income he would lose should he treat Pickering for free: we were, after all, talking here of two implants to replace the missing front teeth, at a cost of a thousand pounds plus per tooth. And there was the Barry Manilow jaunt to consider; *that* would set him back the best part of five hundred quid when the tickets and the overnight stay and drinks and the rest had been paid for. Add to that the fact that not a single one of his team mates, by their own admission, would be able to offer Pickering their services free of charge, and it quickly became a no brainer. So he charged his normal fee and saved his tears.

Pickering, his dental problems taken care of for the time being, took a taxi to Woodside Auto to ascertain what the damage to his car amounted to. The garage owner informed him, with much sucking in of breath and worried frowns, that even though on the face of it the damage didn't amount to much the cost of repairing it amounted to a lot; after all, this is a Beemer we're talking about, this isn't a Ford, squire, this is quality German engineering we have here. On questioning the garage owner further Pickering was assured that the repairs could be carried out that day, but at a price. Rather than go home and have to return, and as he hadn't yet had a good look round Middleham and now was as good a time as any, Pickering chose to pay that price, stay in a hotel overnight and pick up the car the following morning.

*

By eight-o-clock the same morning Duckworth and the rest of the Upper Medlock cricket team had put their plan, hatched in *The Grim Jogger* the previous evening, into action.

Duckworth and Scrivener had done their work well and every member of the team attended the meeting. After opening the proceedings Duckworth made known his grave suspicions that something was going on at The Olde Mill

Cottage, he didn't know exactly what, but whatever it was it was bound to be dirty work and certainly wouldn't be to the benefit of the Upper Medlock Cricket team if he knew that twat Marchbank. The purpose of the meeting was to apply their collective brainpower to the problem with a view to coming up with what precisely was going on there and what they were going to do about it. He had high hopes of Potts - who regularly finished the Sun crossword and wasn't bad at Sudoko either - coming up with something.

"And don't say 'Search me'," he ended, with a sidelong glance at Scrivener. "I've already had more 'Search me's' than I can handle; Search me's' are going to get us precisely nowhere."

After a moment or two's silence with everyone deep in thought, though not necessarily about the brooks at The Olde Mill Cottage as Tilly Turner had just walked in with her latest boyfriend and most of her breasts on display, Threlfall said, "Two brooks, you say?"

"Two brooks."

"What does he want two brooks for?"

"Search me," said Duckworth. "Fuck me!" He turned his wrath on Scrivener. "You've got me saying it now see!"

"But now they're filling them in?" said Potts, while Scrivener was still thinking of a suitable reply.

"What?" said Duckworth, still annoyed at Scrivener and only half hearing the question.

"The brooks? They're filling them in now?"

"Right."

"Both of them?"

"Well as far as I know. Why would they fill one of them in and not the other?"

"Have any of you got a power drill you can lend me?"

said Bristow.

"Only I was wondering," continued Potts, and probably saving Bristow's life in the process if the murderous look Duckworth was giving him was anything to go by. "I mean if they only fill in the brook you say they're filling in, and they leave the other one as it is....?" Potts ended the sentence in a questioning tone, inviting Duckworth to arrive at the same conclusion he himself had.

Duckworth didn't.

A little quicker on the uptake than his captain, Threlfall said, "*It will leave The Olde Mill Cottage in Lower Medlock.*"

"Bloody hell!" said Piggy Higginbottom.

"Bloody hell what?" said Duckworth, still not making the connection.

"Well it would mean that Jonny Pickering can't play for us, wouldn't it," said Potts. "It would mean he can only play for Lower Medlock."

"Bloody hell!" said Duckworth.

"If that's what they intend doing," said Potts.

"Oh it's what they intend doing all right," said Duckworth, who needed no convincing when it came to the tricks the Lower Medlock side were capable of pulling. "I don't know why they dug two brooks and now they're filling one of them in but that arsehole Marchbank isn't there watching them do it for nothing." He nodded vigorously. "Yes, that's what they intend doing all right." He got to his feet, rubbing his hands in anticipation as though about to deal with the problem there and then. "Well we'll soon see about that!"

CHAPTER FIFTEEN

Floater
1. A delivery bowled by a spinner that travels in a highly arched path, appearing to 'float' in the air.
2. A turd that refuses, despite all efforts, to be flushed down the lavatory.

In the event Duckworth couldn't deal with the problem immediately as the day had run out of daylight by the time the meeting ended. So it was at dawn the following morning that all the team, with the exception of Gibbon, who had to go to a *Flog It!* valuation day at Margate, descended on the cottage. Armed with an assortment of picks, shovels, forks and wheelbarrows they set about emptying the brook of all the builder's rubble that had been tipped into it by Wilde & Son the previous day. Afraid that the contractor's men, once they arrived on the scene, might use it to fill in the brook again, they transported it fifty yards or so into the woods and dumped it out of sight.

The previous day Wilde & Son had filled in about half the brook but by the time they arrived to complete the job at nine-o-clock Duckworth and company had emptied most of it.

On discovering this, one of Wilde's men, Hawthorne, demanded to know what was going on. Duckworth told him what was 'going on' was that they were removing the rubble that Wilde & Son had dumped in the brook, and that if he and his mate started dumping more rubble in the brook that he, Duckworth, would take great pleasure in dumping them in the brook along with it. Hawthorne phoned the office for instructions. The Upper Medlock task force carried on emptying the brook and had almost finished the job by the time Marchbank arrived to oversee what he fondly imagined would be the completion of the job.

"What...?" Marchbank said, on taking in the scene, the completion of the sentence left unsaid, but which in all probability was 'the fuck is going on' judging from the expression on his face, Marchbank not being a man slow to use expletives when the occasion demanded.

Neither was Duckworth. "Fuck off," he said, when Marchbank approached him and restated his enquiry in full, replacing the surprised tone with a belligerent one. "I know your game, Marchbank, and if you think you can get away with it you've got another think coming."

Unsure of himself, Marchbank drew in his horns a little. Could Duckworth have discovered what the Lower Medlock plan was? He certainly knew something or he and his mates wouldn't be doing what they were doing. He surveyed the scene again as the Upper Medlock captain and his team continued to empty the brook. He was pleased to note that they were getting rid of the rubble somewhere in the woods and not putting it in the other brook, which would have been the obvious place to put it for people who had half a brain between them, as it would have had the effect of putting The Olde Mill Cottage in Upper Medlock. Which meant that they couldn't be fully aware of what the Lower Medlock plan was. However the penny might drop at any time. Before it did Marchbank thought it might be prudent to get Wilde & Son's men back to the job of filling in the brook again.

"But what's the point?" Hawthorne protested, when Marchbank ordered him to do this. "They'll be emptying it out as fast as we can fill it in."

Marchbank glared at him. "You're being paid good money, some of it mine, to fill it in. So do it."

"Besides, they've threatened us with violence if we start filling it in again."

"I'll do more than threaten you with violence, I will commit bloody violence."

Hawthorne shrugged and he and his mate unloaded the truck of its fresh load of rubble and set about dumping it in the brook. As fast as they dumped it in Duckworth and his men shovelled it out and dumped it in the woods. Half-an-hour of this had passed when Wilde appeared on the scene.

"What's going on?"

"You might well ask," Marchbank said. "Your bloody men are so slow that they can't fill in the brook as fast as that low-life Duckworth and his mob are emptying it."

Wilde looked puzzled. "But why are they emptying it?"

"Because they have realised that if it is filled in, if your men ever move their idle arses fast enough to fill it in, that Jonny Picker....Jesus Christ!"

"What's the matter?" said Wilde, alarmed, not surprisingly as Marchbank looked as though he was about to explode.

The matter was that in the meantime Marchbank's worst fears were realised when it dawned on Potts that if they were to dump the stones they were taking from the brook into the other brook, rather than into the woods, that the position viz-a-viz Jonny Pickering playing for one or other of the villages, would be reversed. He took no time in informing Duckworth and Duckworth immediately ordered the men to do just that. Marchbank watched them doing it for all of two seconds then got on his mobile and began ringing round the rest of the Lower Medlock team.

*

By mid-morning there were as many people emptying stones out of the brook on the Lower Medlock side of the The Olde Mill Cottage and dumping them in the brook on the Upper Medlock side as there were men emptying stones out of the brook on the Upper Medlock side and dumping them in the brook on the Lower Medlock side. They comprised of most of the members of both teams, aided and abetted by friends, children, supporters, and in two cases wives, in total a force of getting on for two hundred people, split more or less evenly between the two factions, the Lower Medlock party was augmented by Wilde & Son's men.

At ten minutes past eleven the Lower Medlock contingent was almost depleted by two when Mr Wilde of Wilde and Son turned up, took in the scene, and promptly withdrew his men on the grounds that if they had been left to do the job without interference it would already have been completed. Marchbank was aghast. The Upper Medlock team were already making a far better fist of the job, by virtue of most of them being manual workers of one sort or another, and thus able to go about their task without claiming tiredness and taking a rest every few minutes, which was the situation with the solicitors, accountants and financial advisers etc of the Lower Medlock contingent. Fearful that the situation would slip even further away from him Marchbank quickly re-negotiated the contract, and the Wilde & Son men stayed on.

When they had first set about their mission both the Upper Medlock and Lower Medlock task forces had gone about their work in an unorganised, undisciplined manner, taking a stone or piece of builder's rubble, sometimes a couple of red bricks or a wooden joist, out of one brook and walking with it to the other brook. However shortly after Wilde had departed Potts, possibly with the benefit of having sharpened up his brain by doing the Sun's crossword when they had stopped for a tea break, had had the idea of forming a human chain, stretching from one brook to the other, and passing the stones and rubble from one link in the chain to the next, and so on. The gain in efficiency brought about by this ploy was only slight however, as no sooner had they adopted it than Marchbank and company, the parasitical nature of their brains making up for their lack of manual skills, copied it. The scene, which had previously resembled a large anthill with ants scurrying aimlessly about, now resembled an anthill once the ants had got their act together.

The new method of work proceeded apace, but as before more apace by the Upper Medlock team than by their Lower Medlock counterparts, despite Marchbank continually urging on his compatriots to greater efforts.

About an hour after the human chain method of doing the job had been initiated O'Casey arrived on the scene with his nephews to pick up the pile of stones he had set aside for the wall he was building, a pile of stones that had long since disappeared, having by this time been dumped in one of the brooks. O'Casey, observing this, and also noting that there were lots of other stones there just or the taking, instructed his nephews to take them.

"What's going on now?" said Penrose a moment later, pausing to mop his brow and observing the nephews loading up the truck and O'Casey himself, watching them in a proprietorial manner.

"What?" said Marchbank crossly. Crossly because seconds earlier he had dropped a large stone on his foot and his big toe was letting him know it to some tune.

"Over there see." Penrose pointed at the truck. "Looks like the Upper Medlock lot have drafted in reinforcements."

Penrose's assumption was understandable as the nephews were taking stones from the brook that the Upper Medlock task force was in the process of emptying.

"It's that twat O'Casey and his twats of nephews!" said Marchbank, dropping one of the two red bricks he was in the process of handing to Doyle-Davidson and just about managing to hop clear before it caused further damage to his foot. "You see what your Irish mate is doing now?" he raged at Doyle-Davidson. "Consorting with the bloody enemy."

Doyle-Davidson looked. "It would appear so."

"Appear so my arse; it isn't appearing so, it is so. So what are you going to do about it?"

"I'll have a word with him," said Doyle-Davidson. "Try to talk him into helping us instead, in view of the previous work we put his way."

"The previous work *you* put his way," said Marchbank. "The work you put his way that caused all this trouble in the first place."

A thought then occurred to Doyle-Davidson. "We'll probably have to pay him more than Upper Medlock are paying him of course."

"We will fuck as like," said Marchbank. "We're not paying him anything."

Doyle-Davidson shrugged. "Then I'm afraid there isn't a lot we can do about it."

"No?" snarled Marchbank. This latest development coupled with his throbbing big toe had brought him to the end of his tether. "I'll show you what we can do about." With that he took a couple of steps forward, drew back his arm and hurled the remaining red brick in the direction of O'Casey and his nephews.

Throwing was not one of Marchbank's skills. Well aware of this gap in his cricketing skills he had fielded in the slips ever since he had been appointed captain, a position from where he was still liable to drop any ball that offered itself up for a catch, but from where he had slightly more chance of hitting the stumps when attempting to run out one of the opposition. Even before he had been made captain he had fielded in the slips, once the previous captain had realised that he couldn't hit a cow's arse with a banjo much less hit the stumps with a cricket ball from mid off. Consequentially the brick he hurled at O'Casey and his nephews didn't go anywhere near them.

*

After settling the bill for his overnight stay in Middleham's excellent *Duke of York* hotel Jonny Pickering pointed the nose of his newly-repaired BMW in the direction of the Medlock villages and began the drive home. He drove at a leisurely pace; it was a nice day and he had the hood down, the better to take in the passing scenery; there was no hurry, he might even stop off somewhere en route if he happened upon something that looked as if it might be of interest. Besides, the thought of home wasn't as welcoming a thought as he would have liked; the odds were strongly in favour of one or more of the Upper Medlock team still being on the premises, re-painting the doors or the skirting boards or something else they'd found to paint; or maybe one of them would be outside doing something in the garden or at the walls, or on the roof re-thatching it, or pointing the chimney that someone had given the once-over and decided that it wouldn't stand another winter.

Although perhaps not? How long was it since he'd last seen the inside of The Olde Mill Cottage? Five days? Six? They may all have completed their labours and retreated to their own homes by now and with luck he might be able to get a bit of peace and quiet. He certainly hadn't had very much of it since he'd come to live in this neck of the woods.

As he drove along he totted up his injuries. Two black eyes, thankfully both a lot less black by now, more a lightish mauve, although still a bit puffy. A broken nose, thankfully healing now. Concussion, thankfully gone by now. And the loss of his two front teeth. Nothing to be thankful for there though; the molars were gone forever, soon to be followed by more if that dentist fellow was to be believed.

He asked himself for the hundredth time if he had done the right thing by retiring to Upper Medlock or Lower Medlock or whichever Medlock it was he'd ended up in. Would he have had the attentions of the populace forced upon him if he had chosen one or other of the Lake District villages he had considered? Or one of the Cotswolds or Snowdonia villages he had looked at? He would never know. Check. He *might* know, one day. And a day in the not too distant future. Because if the residents of Upper and Lower Medlock continued to make his life a misery by forcing their unwanted gifts on him, and continued to entreat him to play cricket for them, he would simply up sticks and move to a village in one of the other areas he had considered.

This last thought got him thinking again about his decision to play for Lower Medlock. How would the Upper Medlock side take it? Not very well, he supposed. All right, they wouldn't be so generous with their gifts of free milk and free window-cleaning and all the other free goods and services they had heaped upon him from the moment he'd arrived, but he didn't think for one minute that it meant he had seen the last of them. What would they do about it? What if they turned nasty? He had already sustained multiple injuries when they were being nice to him, what injuries might he suffer if they became hostile? A vision of a man being hanged, drawn and quartered flashed through his mind.

So maybe playing for Lower Medlock in order to teach Upper Medlock a lesson wasn't such a good idea after all? Perhaps it would be better to go along with his original inclination and play for neither of them. What would be their reaction? How would they feel about it if he made it quite clear to them that they would both be wasting their time if they continued to ask him? Or - even better - why not just tell them that he couldn't play for either team after all as the day they wanted him to play he would be away on holiday; he could tell them it had always been so, he'd had the holiday booked all the time, a trip to the Caribbean with an old England colleague to drop in on a few old West Indian cricketing adversaries who had become lifelong friends, he'd completely forgotten all about it, very sorry and all that, thanks very much for asking but no thanks.

But that would mean disappearing from the scene again, if he wasn't to be found out in a lie. Plus he would be faced with the same problem when the match came round again the following year and the years after that. Besides, he would be telling lies, and being anything less than four square was not the Jonny Pickering way. No, he would simply tell both teams that he wasn't going to play for either of them, not only in the forthcoming match but in any future matches, despite anything they might come up with to try to make him change his mind.

He was still thinking this on arriving back at the cottage, observing the manic activity there and wondering what the hell was going on, when the red brick thrown by Marchbank hit him on the side of the head and pole-axed him.

CHAPTER SIXTEEN

The Piggy Higginbottom Affair

When they are children men with the surname Higginbottom are often given the nickname 'Piggy'. It is easy to see how it is arrived at; Higginbottom - Higgy - Piggy. However this is not the case with Jason Higginbottom, the Piggy Higginbottom who plays cricket for Upper Medlock. Jason is known as Piggy because he once fucked a pig.

At the age of fourteen young Piggy had two ambitions in life. The first was to play cricket for Upper Medlock, a goal he would achieve on the date of the first league fixture of the following season. The captain and star batsman of the fifteen-and-under side, he was already good enough for the senior team - everyone in the village who knew anything about cricket said so - but his father, Brian Higginbottom, who was the current captain of the team and protective towards his son, didn't want to introduce him to the hurly-burly of senior cricket before his fifteenth birthday, which would pass during the coming winter.

The timing of the achievement of his second ambition was not so certain. Like most boys of his age Piggy was still a virgin and as such desperate to shed his virginity. Despite having invested all his weekly pocket money for the last two years on gifts of sweets and ice cream to all the girls of his age in the village he hadn't even got near to having sex with a single one of them. The nearest he had come was a feel of one of Gina Jones's bare breasts, and even that small victory was by no means certain as not having had the advantage of feeling a bare breast before he wasn't even sure he had felt it; it had felt more like a bony shoulder and, in the dark of the cinema, could well have been. The breast certainly didn't feel like he expected breasts to feel, didn't feel how it explained that they felt in one of his father's paperbacks, like twin heavenly orbs, soft yet firm, with stiff-standing nipples. As far as he was able to discern in the gloom of the back row of Studio 2 of the Middleham multiplex Gina's breasts didn't have any nipples, let alone stiff-standing ones.

Several of his friends had had sex, or claimed they had. Most of them would be lying, Piggy assumed, like he himself lied whenever anyone asked him. Troy Parkinson had had it - although everyone at school was unsure if it officially counted, as it was with his sister - but Piggy knew for certain that Tommy Boe had had it because he had paid him fifty pence to watch him having it, with the school bicycle, Honor Baxter (inevitably nicknamed 'Honor and off her'). Piggy had asked, even implored Honor to let him have a ride on her too, for the going rate of a Mars Bar, but she had always turned him down, telling him that he was too weedy and it would be a long time before she was in *that* much need of a Mars Bar.

It was in another of his father's books, *The Last Picture Show,* by an American author named Larry McMurtry, that Piggy came across the notion of having sexual intercourse with farm animals. He thought at first it was a joke - he had heard the expression sheep shagger but had never thought for a moment that people actually did shag sheep - but on reading further, and learning that it was boys who were not much older than he himself who were having sex with the animals, he could see why this might well be true, especially if the boys had been as desperate for sex as he was.

He wondered if having sex with a farm animal would be as good as having it with a girl, but even as he wondered knew he had no way of knowing since he'd never had sex with a girl and therefore had nothing to compare it to. So, his search for sex being no nearer to becoming a reality than the day he had set out on what was turning out to be a very long road to finding it, he decided to go down the farm animal route.

He suspected it would be much less of a problem finding a farm animal to have sex with than finding a girl to have it with; there were at least half-a-dozen farms within the boundaries of Upper and Lower Medlock and they all had cows. At a guess he would say there were at least a thousand. Whether one of them would consent to having sex with him with was another matter - there was nothing in Mr McMurtry's book about the difficulty or otherwise of this - Piggy just hoped that they weren't as unforthcoming about it as girls. There was also no indication by the author as to any enjoyment the cows might get from the act, the book concerning itself only with the pleasure the boys derived from the trysts with their bovine inamoratas.

Apart from wondering whether or not Mr McMurtry had written from personal experience or was just the possessor of a very vivid imagination the book had raised several questions in Piggy's young mind. Would having your penis in a cow's vagina, or any other farm animal for that matter, feel the same as having it in a girl? He very much hoped so. Tommy Boe said having it in a girl felt like liquid velvet. Troy Parkinson said the same and added the word 'warm' to an already mind-blowing description. Piggy didn't know what liquid velvet felt like but it sounded very nice, warm or otherwise.

There was also the possibility that cows might be as unwilling as girls to bestow their favours. And even if they weren't, even if cows were up for it, what if there was the cow equivalent of Honor Baxter amongst their herd, a cow which would do it for a handful of grass and a few buttercups with anyone who was prepared to pay the price, but refused point blank to do it with Jason Higginbottom? And should he milk the cow first? Boys played with girls breasts as a prelude to having sex - although all that it had led to the night he might have felt Gina Jones's breasts was a request from her to move his head out of the effing way because she couldn't see the film - so might fondling a cow's breasts be a sort of cow foreplay? And did cows have periods? Several girls had told him they would have been only too willing to have sex with him if only they hadn't been having their period; would cows be the same? He didn't know the answers to any of these questions and more. There was only one way to find out.

That night, as soon as darkness had fallen, Piggy made his way to a field belonging to Farmer Johnson, the owner of the nearest farm to his home. He made the sortie under cover of darkness, fearful that someone might see him - it was one thing having sex with a cow but quite another to be seen having it!

Since reading the sex with farm animals passage in *The Last Picture Show* he had wondered which breed of cow might offer up the best sex - the book didn't give any advice on this

- or whether having sex with one cow was very much like having it with another. However, having observed that boys and men tended to gravitate more towards the pretty ones at the expense of the plain ones, and that there must be a good reason for this, with the possibility that it was because the quality of sex was better, he opted for a Jersey as they were a nicer colour than the others and had big limpid eyes and even longer eyelashes than Kylie Waterhouse.

Farmer Johnson had several Jerseys in his field along with the Friesians and Ayrshires but unfortunately when it came to picking out one of them the cover of darkness ploy worked against him as it was so dark he couldn't distinguish one breed from another. This being the case he settled for the nearest one that was standing up, took up a position behind it, undid his belt and dropped his trousers. He had thought, when contemplating what he was now about to do, that he might have trouble getting an erection, since unlike a girl's vagina a cow's sexual organ usually has the off-putting sight of a generous load of dried shit encircling it. However, although he could certainly smell the shit, he couldn't see it, and was able to dismiss it from his mind by thinking of Christina Aguilera in her red knickers. Giving his penis a few brisk wanks he was erect in seconds. Thus primed he took hold of the cow's tail, for something to hang on to in case it got a bit too frisky, and snuggled up to its bottom.

He realised more or less straight away that things might not be as straightforward as he had thought. In addition to being of slight build Piggy was small for a fourteen-year-old, not much over five feet tall, and even though he had more than his fair share in the penis department - the third biggest in the class when they'd measured them behind the bike sheds, up from fourth place since they compared them a month earlier - it was immediately apparent that the business end of it was still some way from the cow's vagina. He jumped up to see if he could leap high enough to reach the cherished target. On the third attempt he felt the end of his penis make contact, but in doing so realised that he would have to jump a good deal higher if he were to obtain penetration. Could cows be persuaded to bend down a bit? If he could persuade the cow to drop down on its front legs, like they did prior to lying down, then that would be just about right. He paused in thought for a moment. *Was* it cows that dropped to their knees before lying down, or was it camels? He couldn't remember. But even if they did, how do you get them to do it? Was there a command that cowherds used when they wanted a cow to drop to its knees? He tried a commanding "Bend down" in one the cow's ears but its only response was a non-committal "Moo". He tried jumping up again to see if he could manage to jump a bit higher - even the end of his penis in would be nice, and if he could leap high enough to get it in he might be able to haul himself up on its tail and with any luck get the rest of it in. He tried again and failed again. Defeated, exasperated, and wishing he'd tried harder when the games teacher was instructing his class on how to do the high jump last week, he went home to give the problem some thought.

The following night, again under cover of darkness, the benefit of the night skies being even more important than it had been the night before as he was now carrying a mop and a bucket of soapy water and didn't want to risk anyone asking him what he was doing walking about thus armed at nine-o-clock at night. On arriving home the previous evening he had discovered that the light blue shirt, dark blue pullover and grey trousers he was wearing were now a sort of khaki-coloured shirt and pullover and trousers, thanks to their being covered in cow shit, deposited there by his coming into contact with the cow's bottom. His intention in providing himself with mop and bucket was twofold; one, to give the cow's bottom a good swabbing before attempting to have sex with it; and two, to then turn the bucket upside down and stand on it so he was at the correct height to have sex with it.

The first of these ambitions was accomplished, so far as he knew - so far as he knew because due to working in the dark of night he couldn't see the cow properly, and even if he had been able to it wouldn't keep still, possibly because it objected to having its bottom mopped at a quarter past nine at night. There was no doubt about the success or otherwise of the second of his ambitions; it ended in abject failure when he stood on the bucket, discovered that his penis was still a little shy of the target, jumped up a bit in order to reach it and put his feet through the bottom of the bucket when he came down. It took him the next ten minutes to extricate his feet, one of which he thought might have sustained a broken ankle, and at that point he called off the attempt for the second time and limped his way home.

Fortunately the ankle was only badly bruised and four days later he made another attempt at cow heaven. This time he abandoned the idea of cleaning the cow's bottom in favour of wearing his mother's plastic pakamac over his clothes. The bucket was dispensed with in favour of a stepladder. That afternoon on getting home from school he had set up the stepladder in the backyard and climbed to the top step to check if it would bring him up to the required height. It confirmed to him that along with a cow there would be an excellent chance of being able to fuck a giraffe as well, and maybe a elephant, should he so desire. It was all systems go.

Piggy felt the cover of darkness to be just as necessary as it had been before, as although walking through a field of cows with a stepladder was slightly less suspicious-looking than when armed with a mop and bucket it was still fairly suspicious-looking.

Using the stepladder to stand on to have intercourse with a cow turned out to be an excellent idea insofar as it brought Piggy up to the required height concomitant with executing the act, but a bad idea inasmuch as when he was standing on the step that brought him up to the right height the end of his penis was about a foot away, on the other side of the stepladder from the cow's vagina. Not a boy to give up easily Piggy's next strategy was to employ the stepladder as an ordinary ladder, lean it against the cow's rear end, climb up it and enter the cow by that method. In attempting to achieve this he mounted the makeshift ladder successfully, but not the cow, as every time he started to walk up the ladder the weight of him pressing against the cow's behind caused it to move forward, with the result that the ladder crashed to the ground, taking Piggy with it. The third time it happened he trapped his already sore foot between one of the steps and the ground and was again forced to retire hurt.

September 8, 2003.

Upper Medlock v Lower Medlock. Wickets pitched 2pm. Umpires R Montmorency, M Wilks.

Upper Medlock

J J Hopkins b de la Mare 10
J Hopkins jnr c and b Sneed 35

A L Warnock b Sneed 20
G Green run out 17
A Watkins-Thompson lbw b de la Mare 14
B Higginbottom (C) b Springfield 2
M Coffey c Spragg b Taylforth 22
O L Whittaker st Swann b Sneed 0
J Jennison not out 10
B Swindells lbw b Cliff 3
K Gee b de la Mare 0
  Extras 14
    Total 147

Lower Medlock 145 for 2

V Chambers b Jennison 47
R P Roderick not out 70
W Colon c Whittaker b Swindells 18
J Penberthy not out 0
  Extras 10
    Total 145

Match abandoned

Whilst he was waiting for his wounded foot to heal in readiness for another attempt on a cow it occurred to Piggy that a smaller farm animal, one with which he could have sex without the aid of something to stand on, might better serve his purpose. A hen was discounted as being too small and too noisy; a duck, with which to figuratively break his duck, was rejected for the same reason. A local farmer had two pet llamas in his field and although Piggy judged them to be about the right height he wasn't convinced that just because they lived on a farm they could be counted as farm animals. Besides, the only time he had ever got close to one of them it had spat at him and he could do without that, sex or no sex. Sheep too, which were about the right height for purpose if you bent down a bit, were also a non-starter, the Medlock villages being dairy farming country and there not being any sheep to be had and had. There was, however, at least one pig; in fact a conveniently located pig, housed as it was in a corner of the farmer's field adjoining the Upper Medlock cricket ground, a spot Piggy passed most evenings during the cricket season when he was returning home following batting and bowling practice. A pig would be just about the right height; he might have to squat down a little to achieve penetration but he certainly wouldn't have to jump up and down. Furthermore he couldn't foresee any other problems; when he'd looked at the pig with the eyes of a prospective suitor for the first time, rather than with the disinterested glance he occasionally gave it as he passed by, the pig had looked quite placid and accommodating.

This time, to give himself the absolute best chance of success, he decided to eschew the cover of darkness. His reasoning, apart from it being the first time he would be able to see what he was doing ,which he thought must increase his chances by a fair number of per cent, was that it was very unlikely anyone would see him as he planned to do the deed in the covered part of the pig's sty. As a further insurance against being spotted he opted to do it on Saturday afternoon, when it was unlikely there would be anyone about - many of the women in the village would be busy doing the weekly shopping and those who weren't would be with their husbands and children at the annual cricket match against Lower Medlock.

Cometh the hour and Piggy arrived at the pig's sty without incident. Fortunately the pig was in the covered part of its quarters, which saved Piggy the trouble of coaxing it in there with the bag of apples he had brought with him for that purpose, leaving nothing to chance. It didn't even look up when he stepped into the sty, being much more interested in the pile of potato peelings it was noisily munching its way through.

Piggy saw a snag almost immediately. Whereas cows have a long tail the pig had a curly little excuse of a tail, hardly a tail at all; and certainly not tail enough to hang on to. As luck would have it help was at hand in the shape of a short length of rope hanging from a nail on the wall of the sty. Piggy wasted no time in putting it to good use by fashioning it into a halter. Pleased with himself he slipped the halter over the pig's neck, pulled it tight, hooked his thumbs under it to ensure he had a good grip on it, and was ready to go.

Throughout the time Piggy had been doing this the pig remained singularly uninterested. It ceased to be uninterested and became very interested the moment Piggy dropped his trousers and entered it. In fact it was fortunate - or perhaps unfortunate in view of what was to follow - that Piggy was hanging onto the halter, otherwise the intercourse might have stopped from the moment the pig suddenly took off at a rate of knots Piggy had previously not thought possible in a pig.

Whether having one's penis in a pig's vagina is an enjoyable experience Piggy was never to know - it could have felt like liquid velvet or liquid nitrogen or liquid anything as far as he was concerned - when the pig shot out of the sty and into the field he was far too busy trying to disengage himself from it in his efforts to preserve life and limb to concern himself with such matters.

If Piggy had closed the gate behind him on entering the farmer's field instead, in his haste to have sex with the pig, leaving it open, the terrible events that followed would not have happened. They still might not have happened had the pig, on passing through the gate, turned left and ran up the lane that led to the farmhouse. But instead, for reasons best known to itself, it chose to turn right, and that way led only to the cricket ground.

Piggy's father Brian, bowling his off-cutters from the end facing the farm, was the first to see the pig with his son aboard (although at that distance he did not know it was his son at the time). The match was at a critical stage, with Lower Medlock requiring only two more runs for victory. This being the case Roger Taylor, the batsman to whom Higginbottom was bowling, thought he was the victim of yet another example of Upper Medlock gamesmanship when Higginbottom suddenly came to a dead stop in his run up, looked agog, and pointed straight ahead. (Only two years previously one of the Upper Medlock bowlers had done precisely the same thing and when the Lower Medlock batsman turned round to look the bowler had continued his run up and bowled him out.) Taylor, wise to this, wasn't having any of it thank you very much, and remained unmoved and unmoving.

"It's a pig, there's a pig heading straight for you at about a hundred miles an hour!" Higginbottom shouted, waving his arms desperately and pointing in the direction of the pig again.

"Pig my arse, Higginbottom," said Taylor, and stood his ground.

It was the last words he spoke for some time as two seconds later the pig ran into him, knocking him unconscious to the ground and demolishing all three wickets in the process, before continuing on its way. The bails were never seen again. When smelling salts failed to revive Taylor, and the offer from Hopkins of a smell of his jockstrap as a stronger alternative had been rejected by umpire Montmorency, the services of the cottage hospital were called upon once again. Seizing on the situation as a golden opportunity to avoid defeat Higginbottom suggested to the umpires that as a mark of respect the match should be called off. The Lower Medlock captain Jacobs would have none of it and proposed that the umpires should do no such thing, as in all probability Piggy, on seeing the state of the match and certain defeat for his father's side, had done what he had done on purpose. Higginbottom countered this by saying that it was far more likely that his son was an entirely innocent party and had merely been trying to stop a runaway pig. To which Jacobs remarked that if that was the case why was he fucking it with his trousers round his ankles? In the end, more to stop a potential fight than anything else, the umpires abandoned the match as a draw.

Whilst all this was going on the pig had come to an abrupt halt when it ran full tilt into the sightscreen at the bowlers end, rendering itself as unconscious as it had rendered Taylor moments earlier. Whereupon Piggy withdrew from both the pig and the scene, in that order, before awkward questions could be asked.

CHAPTER SEVENTEEN

Outswinger

1. A delivery that curves away from the batsman.
2. A breast that has fallen out of a girl's bikini top whilst out jogging.

Two hours after being felled by the red brick Jonny Pickering emerged from the treatment room of the cottage hospital, his head swathed in a large bandage. Fortunately there was no concussion this time and apart from having a right ear that would have rivalled in ugliness a boxer's cauliflower ear there was no permanent damage. He was still feeling distinctly groggy from the effects of the blow, and another hour's recovery time would have been advisable, but by this time he was sick and tired of hospitals. Even so, he almost did a smart about face when he saw Marchbank and Duckworth waiting for him in the corridor outside.

At the time the paramedics had been loading the unconscious and bleeding Pickering onto the stretcher prior to transporting him to the hospital Marchbank had approached them and insisted he travel with him in the back of the ambulance as it was he who was responsible for

Pickering's condition. On hearing this Duckworth insisted that he too should travel in the ambulance because Marchbank was travelling in it and obviously, as he had already attacked Pickering once, would in all likelihood try to finish him off if he got half a chance. Marchbank turned on Duckworth and warned him that if he wasn't bloody careful with his mouth he would be getting some of the same. One of the paramedics, observing the open hostility between the two, ruled that neither of them would be travelling in the ambulance, and went on to say that if they were so concerned about Pickering they should make their way to the hospital under their own steam. Marchbank had no alternative but to do this as he wanted to get his story in first before Duckworth got to him. Duckworth had no alternative but to go because Marchbank was going, and needed to be on hand when he inevitably tried to bluff his way out of it.

"Jonny!" said Marchbank in delight, leaping up off his chair in effusive greeting the moment Pickering came out of the treatment room. Then, noticing the look of sheer terror that had suddenly leapt to Pickering's face, a look that would have done credit to a rabbit suddenly encountering a dozen ferrets, he quickly went on, "About the brick. One of the Upper Medlock lot was about to attack you. I was merely trying to stop him."

"You bloody liar!" said Duckworth.

Pickering, despite feeling groggy, had done quite a bit of thinking whilst he was being treated, most of it, again, about the injuries he had sustained since moving into The Olde Mill Cottage not much more than a week previously, and how he had had his more than his fill of them already and didn't want to court any more. It was clear to him that all the wounds had been caused directly or indirectly by members of the Upper and Lower Medlock cricket teams; the only injury he had been unsure about was the loss of his front teeth, but it had since been made obvious, from the scene that greeted him on his return from Middleham, that they were complicit in that too.

He took a moment to compose himself, and then said, with no little effort, for he was a man who would far prefer to turn the other cheek rather than risk any unpleasantness, "I have no intention of playing cricket for either of your teams. Ever."

*

When Marchbank and Duckworth returned to The Olde Mill Cottage everyone there, unsure as to what to do in the light of what had happened to Pickering, had done nothing, and had eventually made their way home. On discovering this both men were about to do the same when Pickering himself arrived in a taxi. In deference to him, probably in the hope that a show of respect might store up brownie points in support of any future pleas they might make for him to change his mind, they stood by as he paid off the taxi and made for the cottage. Short of the brook he stopped, looking into the near distance, and turned to Duckworth and Marchbank in surprise. "Is that *another* brook at the back of the cottage?"

"Him and his mob are responsible for that," said Duckworth immediately, indicating Marchbank.

"We thought you'd like two, Jonny," said Marchbank. "But we'll fill one of them in if you like," he added quickly. "Or both of them if you prefer. Willingly."

Pickering surveyed the scene. "It looks to me like you already are filling in both of them."

"Er....yes," said Marchbank. "You see we had second

thoughts about the question of your liking a brook and...."

Duckworth interjected. "Two brooks."

"....two brooks. So we were going to fill them in then ask you if you wanted them. I can get my men to carry on doing just that first thing in the morning?"

"Mine can do the same," said Duckworth.

"No," said Pickering quickly. "No, I quite like the idea of having two brooks."

"Exactly what I thought, Jonny," said Marchbank unctuously.

"So did I," said Duckworth.

Pickering started to walk on but a thought caused him to pause. "If you wish to do anything at all for me you can clear the brooks of all the stones and stuff you've been dumping in them."

"But of course, Jonny. I'll get my chaps on it right away," said Marchbank.

"So will I," said Duckworth.

Pickering took another couple of steps towards the cottage then stopped and turned to them. "Of course that doesn't mean to say I will ever play for either of your cricket teams."

"We wouldn't dream of trying to get you to, Jonny," said Marchbank.

"Neither would we, Jonny," said Duckworth.

*

The following night in *The Dun Cow*, at an emergency meeting called by Marchbank, the Lower Medlock captain said, "All right, I'm looking for new ideas to get that bastard Pickering to play for us." At the same time, in *The Grim Jogger*, at a similar emergency meeting, Duckworth was saying exactly the same thing.

CHAPTER EIGHTEEN

The Flog It! Affair

Until July 2012 nobody in the Lower Medlock side knew that Wayne Gibbon was a huge fan of *Flog It!* They still wouldn't have known if Gerard Northcott, a resident of the village, and himself a keen fan of the programme, hadn't dropped into his local for a couple of pints the Friday evening after attending a valuation day at Dover, following which he had regaled the landlord with details of the excursion. During the long wait in the queue to have his Clarice Cliffe ginger jar valued Northcott had apparently got talking to the man seated next to him clutching the World War II German helmet and restored Moorcroft vase. The man, it turned out, lived not a mile from him. Who would have credited it, all that distance away in Dover? What a small world. What's more the man had turned out to be an even bigger fan of *Flog It!* than he himself was, and that was saying something. Evidently he had been all over England and Wales and nearly all of Scotland, and had hardly missed a *Flog It!* valuation day within three hundred miles of Upper Medlock since he'd become interested in antiques four years ago. Pleasant young man he was too, if a bit limited in conversation, name of ....what was it now....? Gibbon, yes that was it, Wayne Gibbon.

Even then nobody in the Lower Medlock side might ever have known that Gibbon was a huge fan of *Flog It!* had not Northcott's local been *The Dun Cow*; and he had been telling the tale of his trip within hearing distance of Jerrold Marchbank.

September 8, 2012.

Upper Medlock v Lower Medlock. Wickets pitched 2pm. Umpires J Roebuck, T Unwin.

Upper Medlock 156 all out

L Duckworth b Sturgess 23
A M Bristow c Penrose b de la Mare 14
J Higginbottom c Marchbank b Sturgess 53
F Francis b Parson 0
S S Spragg run out 8
S Eckersley and b de la Mare 21
A Scrivener lbw b Flatley 0
J Threlfall c Sturgess b Flatley 14
P A Potts b Roderick 12
Woo Sang not out 0
W Gibbon b de la Mare 0
  Extras 11
    Total 156

Lower Medlock 158 for 3.

J Marchbank lbw b Threlfall 42

A Doyle-Davidson lbw b Torrance 27
P Penrose b Threlfall 12
Rev G Green not out 33
D de la Mare not out 30
Extras 14
Total 158

The match had unfurled much as expected until the commencement of the Lower Medlock innings. During the Upper Medlock innings the Lower Medlock bowlers had performed with their usual mix of barely average bowling. The Upper Medlock batsmen had matched it with their usual mix of less than barely average batting, with the exception of Jason Higginbottom, who had batted admirably for his half century despite constant jeers of 'Pig poker' from an element of the Lower Medlock support and enquiries as to whether he had been makin' bacon lately. It was at that stage that the Upper Medlock team, for reasons at the time unclear, took the field with only ten players, the player missing from their ranks being Wayne Gibbon: for it was then, following another excellent buffet during the tea interval - the ladies doing them proud yet again with a Gloucestershire Old Spot hog roast - that the Upper Medlock star bowler was nowhere to be seen.

His team mates, led by a worried and increasingly angry Duckworth, had searched everywhere. In the pavilion, outside the pavilion, in the car park - Gibbon's car was still there so he hadn't gone off somewhere - the perimeter of the ground, the immediate vicinity outside the ground, the bar of *The Grim Jogger* to see if he had gone there to fuel himself with a couple of pints of Old Stumpy for the task ahead - which he had been known to do in the past - everywhere they could think of, but there was no sign of him. Lord Lucan didn't make a better job of disappearing.

"Where the hell could the man have got to?" said Duckworth, removing his cap and scratching his head as though that might help.

"Search me," said Scrivener.

"Those Mediterranean spiced sausage rolls were very nice, weren't they," said Bristow.

Duckworth suspected foul play. In his considered opinion it wasn't beyond the bounds of possibility, in their thirst for victory, that one of the Lower Medlock team had murdered Gibbon. The Reverend Green in the dressing room with a cricket stump being a likely suspect. Or failing that had kidnapped him or had him kidnapped, possibly by the IRA; wasn't their man Roderick of Irish ancestry? Duckworth proceeded to collar Marchbank and said as much. The Lower Medlock captain eyed his opposite number with cold contempt, gave a mirthless laugh and told him he was paranoid.

"Well *something* has happened to him," said Duckworth.

"What's happened to him is that he's realised that your lot have no chance of victory and cleared off out of it to save himself the embarrassment of ignominious defeat," said Marchbank.

"Probably to engage himself in something he has more chance of winning," said Penrose. "Like buying a winning ticket for *Euro Millions*."

"Don't talk like a twat," said Duckworth.

"Is that the tinkle of a bell I hear?" said Penrose, ignoring the jibe and cupping a hand to his ear on hearing the signal for the end of the tea interval.

"Perhaps Gibbon has started selling ice cream?" suggested Marchbank. "Gibbon's Ices."

"Oh I hope so, I quite fancy a pistachio," said Penrose. "Stop him and buy one."

"I fancy a Ninety-Nine myself, who's buying?" said Marchbank.

With a supreme effort Duckworth ignored the Lower Medlock pairs' goading and went in search of the umpires to ask if they could delay the start of the Lower Medlock innings until Gibbon could be found. Umpires Roebuck and Unwin grudgingly allowed a further five minutes. If they had allowed five hours Gibbon might just possibly have been run to ground, for by then he was well on his way to Cambridge.

Just over half-an-hour earlier, at the fall of the ninth wicket, Gibbon had strode from the pavilion in his usual no-nonsense manner and taken his place at the crease. While he was taking guard from Umpire Roebuck Penrose, fielding at first slip, said to the wicketkeeper Roderick, "You'll soon be on your way, Rodders; I can't see this one troubling the scorers." It wasn't in the script to say that Gibbon wouldn't be occupying the crease for very long but Penrose couldn't resist the taunt as Gibbon had bowled him first ball on the last two occasions the sides had met and wanted to get a bit back. Gibbon was about to remind Penrose of his recent record against his bowling, and add that he would soon be taking great pleasure in matching it a third time, when Roderick replied, "Yes. Should give me plenty of time to make that re-arranged *Flog It!* valuation day."

All thoughts of bowling out Penrose first ball disappeared from Gibbon's mind to be instantly replaced with pictures of himself on television alongside Paul Martin at a *Flog It!* auction day. He whipped round to Roderick. "Did you just say there was a *Flog It!* valuation day today?"

"Yes. A late addition apparently. Cambridge. You're

not a fan of the show are you?"

Thirty seconds later the Upper Medlock innings closed. Gibbon was bowled first ball, not offering a stroke. To offer a stroke would have meant he might have hit the ball, an occurrence that was the last thing he wanted. If the ball had happened to miss his wicket his contingency plan was to step backwards on to the stumps and be given out that way. Anything rather than stay a moment longer than necessary.

During the thirty seconds that passed between Roderick asking Gibbon if he was a fan of *Flog It!* and the latter losing his wicket it had been established that Gibbon was indeed a fan of the programme, whereupon Roderick had generously offered him a lift to the valuation day; he was leaving immediately after the close of the Upper Medlock innings, his captain had graciously given him permission to attend. Gibbon needed no persuading. After making short work of leaving the field, and not even pausing to change out of their whites, the two antiques enthusiasts screeched out of the car park in Roderick's Jaguar. And, after a very brief stop at Gibbon's home to pick up his German helmet and Moorcroft vase, were speeding on their way to Cambridge, some thirty miles distant.

There was of course no *Flog It!* valuation day at Cambridge. Neither at the Guildhall, Roderick's first port of call, where he expressed great surprise on finding out that the programme wasn't being recorded there, nor at King's College, nor at any of the other seven Cambridge venues they pitched up at in the hope that it might be taking place there. After the eighth, and Roderick effuse with apologies, they gave up and returned to Upper Medlock. But by the time they arrived back the match was long over.

The following day Duckworth, beside himself with

rage on finding out why Gibbon had disappeared, informed him that he would never play for Upper Medlock again. And the day after, once he had admitted to himself that without his star bowler it would be quite some time before Upper Medlock beat Lower Medlock again, told Gibbon that he had only been joking, and by way of an apology would he care to accompany him to *The Grim Jogger* for a pint or two, on him.

CHAPTER NINETEEN

Dead Rubber
1. A term used in cricket parlance to describe a match in a series where the series result has already been decided by earlier matches.
2. A used condom.

"I'll vote for any idea that doesn't involve filling in brooks with builder's bloody rubble," said de la Mare, with feeling. "Look at the state of these, they're as rough as hell." The merchant banker held up his sore hands so that the rest of the Lower Medlock team sat around their usual table in *The Dun Cow* could see them. As the vast majority of them were unused to using their hands for anything more physical than shaking the hands of clients, with the consequence that they too now had hands that were sore and red rather than their usual soft and pink, de La Mare's words drew several noises of sympathy.

"I'll vote for that," said Flatley. "My back is killing me too."

"And mine," said Sneed.

"My knees are...." Doyle-Davidson started, but was

interrupted by Marchbank before he could go any further.

"Never mind your knees," he said impatiently, then, with a look that spelled out to the assembled company that he wouldn't take kindly to any more complaints, "Or sore hands and bad backs. Kindly stick to the matter at hand. Which is how to get Pickering to play for us."

"Let's have a recap," said Penrose, when it soon became obvious that Marchbank wasn't about to be snowed under with suggestions. "What have we tried in order to get Pickering to play for us thus far?"

"Well we had Blackbottom Brook diverted to put his house in Lower Medlock," said Marchbank. He shot Doyle-Davidson a look that might have killed him if the light in *The Dun Cow* had been good enough for the chartered surveyor to see it. "Or at least we would have done if someone hadn't got that reprobate O'Casey to do the job. But apart from that...."

"I wanted to get the job done as...."

Doyle-Davidson's protest died in his throat as Marchbank dismissed him with an impatient wave of his hand.

"*But apart from that....*it has been the Upper Medlock lot who have been coming up with the ideas. They've done all manner of things for him."

"But without much in the way of success, apparently," said Flatley.

"Which doesn't mean to say that they won't succeed going forward."

"Granted. However, as has already been determined, Duckworth and his motley crew are in a much better position to offer their services for free," said Roderick. "Whereas we are not so fortunate in that regard. I've already made the point that people only want their accounts computing once a year, you might recall."

"And I think I said that my services are only required the once," said Sturgess. "Otherwise...." The undertaker spread his hands in a wordless way of saying he would have dearly loved to do more if only he could.

"On the other hand," said Penrose, as pleased as Punch with himself, "I have assured Pickering that I'll be giving him a generous discount on the four implants he'll be needing." Since examining Pickering the dentist had added to the total of teeth needing replacement the two perfectly good teeth at either side of Pickering's two missing ones. It would double the cost but Penrose wasn't too fussed about this as the generous discount he would be giving Pickering was only five per cent.

"Yes well you're a dentist," said Doyle-Davidson. "It's all right for you."

"Well I don't know what we can do, I'm sure," said Roderick with a shake of his head, after more silence.

"Nor do I," said Flatley.

"Frankly I don't know see what we're fannying around for," said Colon, putting a hand to his mouth as if to stifle a yawn bought on by his compatriots lack of guile.

They all looked at Colon and waited for him to go on.

The ex-police inspector obliged. "It's quite simple," he began.

"Yes but locking him up isn't the answer," said Marchbank before Colon could continue, recalling the policeman's previous solution to the problem.

Colon smiled. "There *are* other methods. Methods that will not only ensure that he doesn't play for Upper Medlock but will ensure that he plays for Lower Medlock. Methods I have used in the past that are guaranteed to get a result. Tried and tested *police* methods."

"Torture?" said Marchbank tentatively. As a solicitor the Lower Medlock captain had heard rumours about the more extreme measures used by Colon in his pursuit of applying the law, rumours he had no trouble in believing if the physical state of some of the defendants he'd seen hauled into court was anything to go by.

Colon paused for a second or two before answering, as though perhaps toying with the idea that torture might be an even better way of dealing with the Pickering problem, before saying, "Blackmail."

"Blackmail?"

Colon nodded.

"What has he done?" said Doyle-Davidson

"Nothing as far as I know," said Colon. "But everyone has got something to hide." No one in the company seemed inclined to argue with this. "But even if they haven't, things can be *arranged*. In this case, time being of the essence, and on the slim chance that Pickering hasn't got something to hide, I am quite sure we will be able to concoct something."

*

"Well I don't see what else we can do, we've tried just about everything," said Higginbottom.

At the same time Marchbank and company were pondering the question of how to get Pickering to play for them the Upper Medlock team were in *The Grim Jogger* wrestling with the same problem.

"I've already re-thatched his roof," said Scrivener, nodding his agreement. "I can't re-thatch it again."

"You could if we set fire to it," said Francis.

"Set fire to it?" said Duckworth.

"Smoke the bugger out."

Duckworth regarded Francis with an expression of long-suffering. He said, as patiently as he could manage under the circumstances, "There isn't a problem with getting him out of the house, Franny; the problem is getting him to play for us once he's out of the house."

"Desperate times call for desperate measures," said Francis.

"We aren't so desperate we have to set the poor bugger's roof on fire," said Scrivener.

Duckworth wasn't so sure. "We are," he said gloomily. "And I'd set it on fire if I thought for one minute it would do any good. I mean the game is only two weeks away and we're no nearer getting him to play for us than the day he arrived here."

Save for the slurping of pints of Old Stumpy there was complete silence for a time, then Robinson said, "How about Billy Ringrose?"

Duckworth frowned. "Billy Ringrose?"

"He lives on Cote Lane."

"Yes I know who he is, Robbo. He's played for us a time or two. When he wasn't in gaol."

"Well he's out of gaol now. He came out a couple of days ago."

"Well that's handy to know. I can get him to play for us if certain people decide to swan off to *Flog It!* whenever it takes their fancy," he continued meaningfully, with a dirty look at Gibbons. "But the purpose of this meeting is to find a way of getting Pickering to play for us."

"That's what I'm doing. We could make Pickering the gift of Billy."

"Make him the gift of Billy?"

"You know, like when I suggested we made him the

gift of Tilly Turner; we could make him a gift of Billy."

Duckworth scoffed. "Billy's gay isn't he. What would Pickering want with him? Pickering isn't gay."

"How do you know? All right, he doesn't look gay. But neither did Rock Hudson. So he could be. I mean he never showed any further interest in Tilly after the time we fixed him up with her, did he?"

"I think her breaking his nose might have had something to do with that, Robbo," said Duckworth.

"We should offer him Beyoncé," said Francis. He spoke this with a wistful air, probably picturing the American chanteuse as he said it. "If he had a night with Beyoncé he'd do anything for us."

"Yes, good idea, Franny," said Duckworth. "And while she's about it we'll get her to set fire to his roof, just in case."

"I was only saying," said Francis, peeved.

"Well don't, unless you've got anything sensible to say."

"Here's a thought," said Potts after a moment. "Billy Ringrose, apart from being...."

Duckworth flashed Potts an angry look. "And I don't want to hear any more shit about Billy Ringrose!"

"Billy Ringrose, *apart from being* a *homosexual*," Potts persisted, determined to make his point, "*is a burglar.*"

"He can't be a very good one if he's just got out of nick for it," said Higginbottom pragmatically.

"He's good enough," said Potts. "For our purposes."

"Our purposes?" said Duckworth. "What are you talking about, our purposes?"

"We could get him to burgle Pickering."

"And how is that going to help?"

"A lot. If he nicks his cricket memorabilia. Pickering's

house is full of it. The bat he scored a triple-century with against the Aussie's at the WACA. The ball he did the hat-trick with against the Indians at Headingley. Silverware. He's got cups and trophies by the dozen."

"Potty's right," said Threlfall. "I noticed that when he invited me in for a cup of tea when I was doing his garden."

"He's got cricket stuff all over the place," said Spragg.

"I didn't know Rock Hudson was gay," said Bristow.

"What's more he's really proud of it," said Spragg.

"Who, Rock Hudson?"

"I was talking to him one day about it," Spragg went on, ignoring Bristow and possibly saving his life judging from the way Duckworth was eyeing him and shaping his hands into a strangler's grip. "When I was painting his kitchen walls. He said the hat-trick ball and the triple-century bat were priceless."

"All right, so they're priceless," said Duckworth. "But how does Billy Ringrose thieving them get Jonny Pickering to play for us?"

"In gratitude of course," said Potts. "For us lot getting them back for him."

"And how do we do that? Why would Billy Ringrose pinch them and hand them over to us?"

"We'd pay him."

"For what he pinches? It would cost us a fortune if Pickering's got as much stuff as you reckon."

"No, I mean pay him for pinching just the hat-trick ball and the triple-century bat for us. Say a couple of hundred quid. Not bad for a night's work."

"I'll do it for two hundred quid," said Threlfall immediately. "I'd do it for a hundred."

"Yes, I'm sure you would, Justin," said Duckworth.

"But if your burgling skills are anything approaching your wicketkeeping skills you'd probably make a balls of it and get caught. And then Pickering would never play for us."

"But what do you think?" said Potts. "In principle. Well worth a punt if you ask me."

Duckworth took a moment or two to think over the suggestion. "Well it *could* work. We'll have to keep a close eye on Ringrose though, he's a slippery little bugger from what I know of him; he might take our money and hang on to the cricket memorabilia as well."

"No he won't," said Spragg confidently. "I'll see to that. You can leave that with me. I'll go with him. Keep him on the straight and narrow. Besides, he'll need one of us with him to point out the ball and the bat."

Spragg might not have been so confident about his stewardship of Billy Ringrose had he known that the burglar didn't always successfully combine his profession with his homosexuality, a failing that had resulted in his being gaoled on more than one occasion, the last one being when he had been so taken by the photograph of the hairdresser he was burgling that the following day he phoned him up and asked for him for a date.

CHAPTER TWENTY

Runner.
1. A player who is called upon by a batsman who might otherwise need to retire hurt.
2. What you do if you can't pay the bill at a restaurant.

"Tch," said Marchbank, with impatience. "Isn't the bloody man ever going to take a piss?"

"He'll have to sooner or later," said the man by his side, Sneed.

Marchbank's face implied this was far from certain. "I'm not too sure about that, he's only had two tonic waters; two tonic waters aren't going to make a man need a piss."

Marchbank and Sneed had had their target under surveillance for the best part of two hours and so far Pickering hadn't even looked at the gents lavatory, far less visited it; and the prize-giving would have to take place sooner or later, the landlord had already delayed it for an hour by lying to Pickering that the main prize-winner had been delayed. In an effort to get Pickering to consume more liquid Marchbank had already tried getting someone to buy him a pint of bitter but Pickering had graciously declined the offer, saying that he always preferred to remain sober when he was performing an official function.

Although every one of the Lower Medlock cricketers frequented *The Dun Cow* from time to time, most of them often enough to be termed 'regulars', Marchbank and Sneed were the only ones there that evening, apart from Roderick, Marchbank being fearful that Pickering might view any more of the team in attendance as suspicious and maybe fly the coop before their plan could be executed. This didn't, however, mean that there was a shortage of customers in the pub that night, the majority of whom were friends or relations of the cricketers.

Marchbank glanced at Pickering again to see if he'd shown any signs of moving off the high stool at the bar since the last time he'd looked about five seconds ago. He hadn't. It drew another scowl of frustration from the Lower Medlock captain.

When Jonny Pickering had been asked by the landlord of *The Dun Cow* if he could possibly be kind enough to replace the Premier League footballer, who had had to pull out of handing out the prizes at the pub's darts team prize-giving night due to unforeseen circumstances, he had been only too pleased to accept the invitation. He was less pleased on arriving at the pub on noting that Marchbank was amongst those present, but the Lower Medlock captain had merely acknowledged him when their eyes met and had made no attempt to engage him in conversation. Pickering would have been further displeased had he known that *The Dun Cow* didn't even have even a darts team, far less a prize-giving night for it, and that the bogus event was simply a ruse to get him on the premises.

"Check to see if Roderick is still in the bog, we don't

want anything going wrong when Pickering finally does decide to go," said Marchbank.

"I haven't noticed Rodders come out," said Sneed.

"Check, all the same," said Marchbank firmly.

"How much bloody longer have I got to stand here?" said Roderick seconds later when Sneed popped his head round the door of the gents.

"Oh not for very much longer I shouldn't think."

"I mean I'm already getting funny looks from people who've been in a time or two. One of them asked me if I was George Michael."

"I'm sure Pickering will be along directly," said Sneed, trying to sound confident.

"Stood here for the best part of two hours with my dick hanging out; what are people going to think?"

"Maybe they'll think you have prostate trouble," Sneed suggested helpfully. "Apparently my father-in-law has to stand for ages and ages waiting for his pee to come."

"Well get your father-in-law to stand here then."

"I would but he isn't here."

"Anyway, why can't you take a turn?"

"Because I'm taking the photograph, aren't I."

"I can do that," said Roderick, and made to pull up his zip. "Give me the camera, I can take photographs."

"No that's my job, that's settled, fair and square, we drew lots." said Sneed, and quickly closed the door before Roderick could argue the matter further.

"You'll have to offer to show him the gents toilet," said Marchbank, when Sneed reported back.

"What?"

"Offer to show him round the gents."

"Pickering?" said Sneed.

"No the Man in the fucking Moon. Of course bloody Pickering!"

"Why would he want to see the gents?"

"Can you think of a better way of getting him in there?"

"Well no; but, I repeat, why would he want to see the gents toilet?"

"Well I don't know," said Marchbank exasperated. Then, thinking on his feet, perhaps not the most remarkable of his talents, as evidenced by his suggestion, "You can tell him you did the tiling and ask him what he thinks about it."

"What he thinks about the tiling?"

"Tell him if he likes it you can do his bathroom at The Olde Mill Cottage just the same, for free."

"I'm a financial adviser not a tiler," said Sneed sniffily.

"Well take him in the gents and give him some financial advice then," said Marchbank impatiently.

Sneed stood back and addressed an imaginary Jonny Pickering. "*Good evening, Jonny, would you care to accompany me to the gents for a little financial advice?*" He turned to Marchbank. "Just how is that going to sound?"

How it would have sounded will never be known because at that moment Pickering took a sip of his tonic water, put the glass down on the bar top and headed for the gents lavatory.

Marchbank's sigh of relief was huge. "At last!" He turned to Sneed. "Ready?"

Sneed patted the camera in his jacket pocket. "Roger."

"Give him ten seconds. Then...." Marchbank took a photograph with an imaginary camera.... "Click. We'll have the bugger on toast."

Ten seconds later when Sneed flung open the gents

lavatory door he saw that everything was going to plan; Pickering had his hand in the flyhole of Roderick's trousers and Roderick, a horrified expression on his face, had his hands on Pickering's hand as though trying to ward him off. To all intents and purposes it would be construed by an onlooker that Pickering was sexually abusing Roderick, in a public place, and in a gross manner. All that remained was to get photographic evidence. Sneed raised his camera.

Seconds earlier, the moment that Pickering had taken up position alongside him at the gents' urinal, Roderick had emitted a blood-curdling scream. The startled Pickering asked him what was wrong.

"I've got my scrotum fast in my zip," howled Roderick. Looking down at himself he calmed down enough to say, "Please, help me get it out would you? I can't see what I'm doing properly down there."

"Try to keep as still as possible and I'll see what I can do," said the gallant Pickering, and bent to take a closer look.

Moments later, with Pickering still taking a closer look at Roderick's fly, and with every second that passed making it more likely he would discover that he had not got his scrotum caught in the zip, Roderick panicked, grabbed hold of Pickering's hand and thrust it into his groin.

If Roderick had left it at that, the plan may very well have succeeded. But the moment Sneed arrived on the scene, in an effort to make the incident look more realistic, he started to struggle violently whilst holding on firmly to Pickering's hand. And in doing so caught Pickering's index finger in the zip. Pickering howled even louder than Roderick had howled and pulled on his hand in an effort to extricate it. With a spurt of blood and the sickening sound of severing flesh, his finger came free.

Sneed, taken by surprise at the speed it had happened, his reflexes maybe slowed down by the four pints of bitter he'd consumed whilst waiting for his moment, dropped the camera and failed in his mission to photograph the incident.

*

Billy Ringrose had been only too pleased to offer his services when Duckworth and Spragg approached him about the burglary. Not only was he out of funds, having spent the last six months incarcerated at Her Majesty's pleasure, and could well do with an easy couple of hundred pounds, there was the added bonus that Jonny Pickering was his favourite cricketer of all time.

Two nights after the Upper Medlock side had come up with the plan it was put into action. Ringrose, accompanied by Duckworth and Spragg, arrived at The Olde Mill Cottage at three-o-clock in the morning, the best time to commit a burglary Ringrose had advised; too late for people not to have gone to bed, too early for them to have got up. Spragg would accompany Ringrose while he stole the hat-trick cricket ball and the triple-century bat. Duckworth would keep guard outside.

Ringrose, impressively expert, broke into the cottage with a minimum of fuss and an absence of noise. There was a full moon that night and sufficient light illuminated the living room to enable Ringrose and Spragg to see their way around even without the help of Ringrose's pencil torch. Spragg quickly located the triple-century bat and tucked it safely under his arm. He then indicated the door that led to the stairs and Pickering's bedroom beyond, where the cricketer kept the hat-trick ball on a chest of drawers.

Ringrose silently eased the door open. Stealthily, quietly, the two mounted the stairs. On the small landing

Spragg pointed out Pickering's bedroom. Its door was slightly ajar. Ringrose, Spragg in close attendance, tiptoed forward and slowly pushed it open. The moonlight that had aided them in the living room now illuminated the bedroom through the undrawn curtains. From the doorway they could see Pickering in bed, his back to them. Spragg pointed to the chest of drawers on the wall facing the bed. Ringrose aimed the beam of his torch at it. Sitting on top, mounted in a solid silver hand, was the hat-trick ball.

Things had gone like clockwork until then. The mainspring started to play up when Ringrose, instead of tiptoeing stealthily over to the chest of drawers and getting the ball, tiptoed stealthily over to Pickering's bed. And gave up the ghost altogether when Ringrose got into bed with him.

The first thing Jonny Pickering knew about it was when he suddenly woke up to feel two arms encircling his body and someone snuggling up to him. A kiss on the neck and a grateful moan quickly followed. At first he thought he was having a nightmare. Before retiring he had drunk a couple of brandies and taken two codeine tablets to relieve the throbbing pain of the wound in his finger sustained the night before, forgetting completely that alcohol and drugs aren't the best of bedfellows. Neither, to a confirmed heterosexual like Jonny, was the owner of the voice that now whispered breathily in his ear, before playfully biting it, "Don't be shy, Jonny, turn round and give us a kiss."

Pickering sat bolt upright and switched on the bedside lamp. He swivelled round to see a curly-haired blonde man in bed with him. The man smiled, pursed his lips and blew him a kiss. Pickering now became aware that someone else was in the room, near the chest of drawers. As he focused on the figure, Spragg, fearful that Pickering would recognise him, raced forward and smote him round the head with the triple-century cricket bat.

*

"We shall have to invite you to the Christmas party, you're here so often," said Nurse Scrivener.

Pickering smiled ruefully despite himself. "So I'm told." At The Olde Mill Cottage an hour earlier, when the paramedics had brought Pickering back to consciousness, one of them had said the same thing.

The nurse finished dabbing with a cotton swab at the dried blood on Pickering's ear, inspected her handiwork, frowned and said consolingly, "It'll match your other ear; that's something to be thankful for."

"Right."

"I mean at least the skin isn't broken. Just puffiness and bruising. No need for stitches this time. You were very lucky."

Pickering grimaced ruefully. "Yes, it's been a long-standing ambition of mine to be assaulted by a burglar with a cricket bat."

"Aw." Nurse Scrivener smiled sympathetically. "Well at least whoever did it to you had the goodness to phone for an ambulance."

"He must have, it certainly wasn't me."

Nurse Scrivener looked thoughtful. "He probably thought he'd killed you."

It was Spragg who had insisted on calling for an ambulance. Billy Ringrose, not unsurprisingly, had voted otherwise. A broken-hearted Duckworth made the voting two to one in favour.

"There, all done," said the nurse, with a final dab at Pickering's ear. "No need for a dressing. It'll look a bit ugly for a while but it will heal quicker if it isn't covered. Would you like me to phone for a taxi?"

"Please." A thought struck Pickering and he managed a smile. "I wonder if the taxi firm too have a Christmas party they can invite me to? I use them often enough."

Nurse Scrivener smiled back. "You see, you're feeling better already."

"Not really," said Pickering, touching his newly-batted and battered ear gingerly.

"Just trying to put a brave face on it, are you? You will feel better though, in time. When you're back home safe and sound on your little island."

"I suppose I will, when....what?"

"When you're back on your island." Nurse Scrivener explained. "My husband said your cottage is like it's on an island now."

"Oh, the two brooks you mean." The construction of the two brooks seemed a long time ago to Pickering. He pictured them encircling the cottage. "Yes, I suppose it is a bit like an island in a way."

"Lucky you. I've always wanted to live on an island. Remote, cut off from the rest of the world."

It's not remote and cut off enough, thought Pickering.

During the time the nurse had been ministering to him Pickering had more or less decided to leave The Olde Mill Cottage and the Medlock villages behind him and move to somewhere less dangerous, maybe downtown Damascus or whichever African country was currently engaged in bloody civil war. He knew he wasn't going to get any peace until he did, unless the villages' cricket teams suddenly stopped pestering him, and there was little chance of that happening if the last couple of days were anything to go by.

In the couple of seconds he had been conscious after switching on the light Pickering had recognised the burglar who had layed into him with the cricket bat as Spragg, the Upper Medlock cricketer who had painted The Olde Mill Cottage inside and out. What would the Upper Medlock team try next if they were capable of something like that? What would the Lower Medlock team try next after that debacle in The Dun Cow gents toilet? Well, country idyll or no country idyll, he wasn't going to stick around any longer to find out. It would be a great shame; Upper Medlock or Lower Medlock, whatever village it was that he was living in, was quite perfect in every other respect. But enough was enough. The moment he arrived home he would be putting the cottage up for sale. And he wouldn't be hanging around until it was sold either, he would be moving out into a hotel or a guest house, somewhere far away from the Medlock villages and well out of reach of their mad, bad, demanding residents, until such time as he'd decided on which other part of the country he would retire to.

"A desert one would be nice," said Nurse Scrivener wistfully, breaking into his thoughts.

"What's that?"

"Island. A desert island. To live on. Palm trees, pure white sands, azure blue sea lapping gently on the shore." She visualised it. "I can see myself now, sat under a parasol with one of those cocktails in a long glass and ....Jonny?" She stopped, concerned. "Jonny, what is it?"

Pickering was staring blankly into space, the beginnings of a smile on his lips.

"Jonny?" Nurse Scrivener passed a hand in front of his eyes and when this didn't work shook his shoulder. "Jonny, are you all right?"

Pickering blinked as though coming out of a trance. Then he said gratefully, "Thank you Nurse Scrivener. Thank you very, very much indeed."

CHAPTER TWENTY ONE

Tail-ender
1. *A player who bats towards the end of the batting order, usually a specialist bowler or wicket-keeper with relatively poor batting skills.*
2. *Sex on the tailboard of a lorry.*

September 7 2012.

Lower Medlock v Upper Medlock. Wickets pitched 2pm. Umpires S Morgans, W Gerrard.

The entire populations of both villages, the only exceptions being the sick and infirm, turned out to see Jonny Pickering make his debut for Lower Medlock. Pickering himself had demanded it as a condition of his agreeing to play. He needn't have bothered; all but a few of them already attended the annual match more than willingly and the addition of the great Jonny Pickering to the proceedings had rendered the fixture quite unmissable. Just try keeping them away! The only people residing within the boundaries of the villages not aware of the match that afternoon were in the graveyard.

Prominent amongst the spectators were the Chairmen of the Upper Medlock and Lower Medlock Parish councils and their ladies, both officials resplendent in their chains of office; Pickering had expressly demanded that the villages' two leading figures graced the fixture with their presence. Both would have been delighted to attend anyway. The press, in the shape of the sports reporter and the chief photographer of the *Middleham Weekly Echo*, were there, again at Pickering's insistence, as was *West Medfordshire Radio*, who would be broadcasting a ball by ball commentary. The people from regional television were covering the event for their news magazine; Pickering had personally requested their attendance and they had expressed their delight in being asked to come along and report on such a momentous occasion.

The day, bright and sunny with just the lightest of cooling breezes, ideal for cricketers and spectators alike, matched the occasion. The ground itself was in tip-top condition, the splendid summer weather, after the damp start to the year, rendering the greensward in as good a condition as anyone could remember. The wicket itself had been given extra and loving care and attention by groundsman George Abbott. It promised to be true and fast.

The applause from the three thousand plus spectators was deafening as Pickering stepped down the pavilion steps with a broadly smiling Marchbank to open the Lower Medlock innings. The pair were applauded every step of the way to the wicket. Marchbank, in deference to his more illustrious partner, walked a yard or so behind him and joined in the applause by thumping his bat on his pads.

As luck would have it the match was being played at the Lower Medlock ground that year, which dictated that the home side - thanks to a rule, necessary following the double-headed penny disgrace of a few years ago - would bat first. Pickering was grateful for this; although it didn't make any difference to him whether he had a ball or a bat in his hand, given the choice he would have preferred it to be the latter as it was a bat that had been instrumental in finally convincing him that he had to do what a man had to do. It would be poetic justice.

On reaching the prepared strip Pickering, who was to take strike, again at his insistence, took guard from Umpire Morgans. He took his time in noting the Upper Medlock field placings, taking no less care than he would have done had he been batting for England in a final test match against the Australians with each side on two victories and all to play for. This done to his satisfaction he was about to settle in the crease in readiness for the opening delivery when, on apparently noticing a flaw on the immaculately prepared surface, he walked leisurely down the pitch and flattened it with a few thumps of the back of his bat. Under normal circumstances, had one of the Lower Medlock openers done this, there would have been a least one raucous cry of 'Get the fuck on with it you hairy-arsed tosspot' from one of the Upper Medlock contingent, either from one of those on the pitch or from someone in the crowd; but this was the great Jonny Pickering, a man to who demanded their total respect.

Satisfied with his bit of 'gardening' Pickering took his time in walking back, checked the Upper Medlock field setting again and settled in the crease to face Wayne Gibbon's opening delivery. The crowd went completely silent in anticipation. As Gibbon started his run up many of them were wondering whether Pickering would hit the ball for a six or a four. Since it was the first ball a few of them thought he might treat it with more respect and settle for playing it defensively back to the bowler, or perhaps leave it if it was missing the stumps, saving the more crowd-pleasing stuff until he got his eye in. A very few hopeful Upper Medlock fans, mostly schoolboys with the more fanciful imagination that comes with youth, thought the ball might bowl him. Not a soul imagined what did happen.

The day after the abortive burglary Pickering had telephoned Marchbank and Duckworth and asked each of them if they would kindly drop in on him that evening at eight, he had something of importance to say. So that it wouldn't come as a surprise to them, and maybe fearful that, like the last time they had met at The Olde Mill Cottage, they might take to fisticuffs, he forewarned them that their opposite number would be there.

"I have decided which one of your teams I shall play for," he said, once he had settled them in two of the cottage's easy chairs and provided each man with a drink.

"Oh?" said Marchbank, with a look of surprise and expectancy; surprise because he had imagined that there was no way on earth the ex-England captain would play for either team following the events of the past couple of weeks, expectancy because if Pickering were indeed to play he was confident that his choice of team would be Lower Medlock.

"Go on?" said Duckworth, with just a look of surprise on his face, all expectations of Pickering ever playing for Upper Medlock having been abandoned after the failure of the burglary, after which Spragg had reported that he was ninety-nine per cent certain Pickering had recognised him.

"I shall play for both teams," said Pickering.

"Both teams?" said Marchbank surprised.

"Both teams?" said Duckworth, equally surprised and almost in unison, so that it sounded like an echo.

"I shall play for Upper Medlock one year and Lower Medlock the following year. And so on." He looked at them keenly. "If that is all right with both of you?"

It was all absolutely all right with both of them, both realising that Pickering's presence in their team would almost certainly guarantee a win. Granted, by the same token it would almost certainly guarantee a win for the opposition the following year, but a guaranteed win once every two meetings, whilst by no means being ideal, was a far better proposition than the humiliation of losing to them two, three, even four times in succession, which had often been the case in the past.

"Who will you play for first, Jonny?" said Duckworth, and answered his question without waiting for a reply. "Upper Medlock, obviously."

"Oh I think you should play for Lower Medlock first, Jonny," said Marchbank immediately. "After all it was I who asked you first."

"Oh bollocks to that," said Duckworth. The Upper Medlock captain was about to list the many things his team had done for Pickering since his arrival, with the exception of maiming him, and the paucity of things Lower Medlock had done for him, but before he could Pickering spoke again.

"I shall toss a coin." He produced a pound coin from his pocket. "Heads I will play first for Upper Medlock, tails for Lower Medlock." As an afterthought, by this time knowing his men, he added, "And I'd be grateful if there was no talk of best out of three after the toss."

With that he tossed the coin high into the air, caught it with one hand and placed it with a resounding slap on the back of the other.

Now, just short of two weeks later, Pickering readied himself as Gibbon broke into his run up. But not to deal with Gibbon's delivery. For when the bowler was about five or so yards from the wickets Pickering straightened up from his batting stance, stepped to one side and held out a protective arm, the flat of his hand facing Gibbon in the approved manner of a batsman requesting a bowler to pull out of his delivery.

As Gibbon slithered to a halt Pickering produced a mini battery-powered loud hailer from his trousers pocket. He switched it on, put it to his mouth and spoke into it: "Attention! Attention please. Can I please have everyone's attention for a moment?"

At the other end Marchbank exchanged puzzled glances with Gibbon.

The Lower Medlock players exchanged puzzled glances. "What's all this about?" said first slip Eckersley to second slip Robinson.

The spectators exchanged puzzled glances. "They're not drawing the raffle already are they?" said one man, hurriedly reaching into his pocket for his ticket.

Pickering spoke to Marchbank. "If you would care to join me, Mr Marchbank?"

Completely non-plussed, Marchbank stepped over to Pickering. Pickering turned to Duckworth who was fielding at gully. "You too, Mr Duckworth, if you please."

Duckworth, equally puzzled, made his way over to Pickering.

Pickering addressed the crowd again. "Can you all hear me clearly? Wave if you can hear me."

The entire crowd waved.

"Can the radio, television and newspaper people all hear me?"

There were affirmative waves from the media.

"Excellent." Pickering then turned his attention solely

to Duckworth and Marchbank. "Gentlemen, a question for you. Is it a fact that only men born in, or currently resident in, Upper Medlock or Lower Medlock, may play for their cricket teams? Mr Duckworth?"

Duckworth, wondering just what was going on, shrugged. "Well, yes. That's the rule."

Pickering turned to Marchbank. "Mr Marchbank?"

Marchbank took a moment before answering. Like Duckworth he hadn't a clue what Pickering was up to, but, a more devious man, knew he was up to something. However not knowing what that something was he had no alternative but to answer. "Yes. That is the case I believe."

Pickering addressed the crowd again. "Did everyone hear that? Wave if you did, please."

There were shouts of "Yes" and waves from the crowd and the media representatives.

Pickering continued. "In that case, as only those men either born or currently resident in either Upper Medlock or Lower Medlock can play for their cricket teams - as you have all just heard Mr Duckworth and Mr Marchbank confirm - I am afraid that I can never play for either. For I live in neither. I live on an island. Between the two villages."

With that Pickering took off his batting gloves, tucked them under his arm along with his bat, and walked from the field with a lighter step than he had walked with for weeks.

EPILOGUE

Reverse Sweep.
1. A stroke played by dropping to one knee and reversing one's hands, enabling a sweep of the ball from leg to off, rather than the more natural off to leg.
2. A homosexual chimney cleaner.

After leaving the cricket field Pickering spent the rest of the day at The Olde Mill Cottage leisurely catching up with his mail, pausing every few minutes to thank his lucky stars, and breaking off once to phone his thanks to Nurse Scrivener, the unwitting answer to his problems when she had mentioned that he now lived on an island. A huge bouquet of flowers and an equally large box of chocolates were already on their way.

The morning of the following day was spent reading the Sunday newspapers and peacefully fishing in one of his new brooks, whilst the afternoon, following the sun, was spent peacefully fishing in his other new brook. As he fished he toyed with the idea of having a small bridge built over the brook at the front of the cottage. It would enable him to drive his car onto the property and park it in the garage, which he hadn't been able to do since the introduction of the brooks. However he quickly dismissed the idea as the establishment of a bridge connecting the cottage with Upper Medlock might be construed as changing the cottage from its island status to its previous designation of being in both Upper Medlock and Lower Medlock, the very last thing he wanted.

The evening was peacefully spent in the gardens with a pair of binoculars spotting the many birds which abounded in the woods surrounding the cottage.

It was the last peaceful pastime he was to have at The Olde Mill Cottage, indeed the last of any peace, as the first thing on Monday morning men and machinery from Wilde & Son commenced to filling in one of the brooks. Half-an-hour later men and machinery from O'Casey & Nephews started filling in the other brook. Pickering put two and two together, got four, and phoned the local estate agency with instructions to put The Olde Mill Cottage on the market forthwith. Two hours later he was packed and gone, never to return.

It took him three weeks to find the ideal place in which to continue his retirement; the village of Higher Ernbeck in North Yorkshire. As with his previous choice of area to retire to it had everything he needed and very little he didn't; a rolling landscape in whose verdant hills and valleys he might take long relaxing walks; two RSPB bird reserves within easy travelling distance; plus the River Ern, which apart from being beautiful had excellent fishing, both salmon and trout. And should he by some strange chance become temporarily bored with rural life the sea, with its bracing air and beaches, was only twenty miles away. However the most ideal thing about Higher Ernbeck, the item right at the very top of his list, was that it didn't have a cricket team.

Bright and early the morning after he moved in there was a knock on his front door. The man on the doorstep introduced himself as Seth Oldthwaite. He welcomed Pickering to the village and told him that they were soon to start up a cricket team and asked if Jonny would please play for them.

Also in paperback by Terry Ravenscroft

THE RING OF THE LORD

Tunnbledemere, the chieftain of Dreg, rose from his ceremonial throne and slowly approached his son Draybweevil. From his robes he produced a silver pendant which he offered to Draybweevil, saying, "Take this sacred pendant, my first born."

Draybweevil's jaw dropped in astonishment. He knew of the sacred pendant but had never seen it before. It was all he expected and more. A long moment passed as he admired its great beauty, then he tore his eyes away, looked deep into the wise, wizened face of his father, a picture of himself in years to come, and said, "The sacred silver pendant of Goz!"

Tunnbledemere smiled fondly at his blond-haired son. "Put it on, good Draybweevil."

With trembling hands Draybweevil took the sacrosanct solid silver pendant and placed it round his neck.

Tunnbledemere continued. "It will help protect you throughout your perilous journey through the Underworld to.... who knows where? Perhaps through Sablon, through Zariam, through Xerezz and Onandonandonandon,"

Draybweevil's ice-blue eyes were already afire with zeal. His breathing quickened. "And my quest, Father?"

Tunnbledemere's tone was solemn. "It pains me to place such a great responsibility on your young shoulders, Draybweevil."

"Young shoulders they may be, Father." His back stiffened. "But broad enough I'll vouchsave."

Tunnbledemere nodded then took the deepest of breaths, as though to invest his words with the seriousness he felt they deserved. "Your quest then, Draybweevil, is.... *nothing less than to find out why everyone in fantasy novels has a silly name!*"

A collective intake of breath came from all those present that fateful day. Gasps of awe, of wonder, of trepidation, were forced from the throats of Binglebang, of Meelamoola, of Bootyscoot, of Snotwangler, of Fartwurgler, of Bumsucka....

Amazon Reader's Review
"Never stopped laughing from beginning to the end, read the last 20 odd pages at around 5 in the morning, and woke my beautiful wife up with my outbursts of laughter, good thing she is very understanding, let's hope there is a follow on. Highly recommend." - JOHN.

STAIRLIFT TO HEAVEN

The 2012 Paralympic Games are still six years away but already the sixty-five year old Terry Ravenscroft is putting together a team for the Throwing the Zimmer Frame competition (should such an event be included). And when he can fit it in. For this is a man who has many other things that fill his waking hours (of which he has more to fill than most people, thanks to the troublesome prostate gland that wakes him up for a pee about six times every night).

Stairlift to Heaven, the journal of an old age pensioner, is an irreverent, hilarious look at one man's life after retirement. Although written by an old age pensioner, non-coffin dodgers should not be put off by this. Everyone will be old someday, and there are valuable lessons in coping with old age to be learned here. Be advised on how to cope with the multitude of maladies that continually bedevil old age (including the aforementioned prostate gland problem and the countless bladder examinations it brings with it); learn how to cope with increasing forgetfulness; how to become adept at dealing with junk mail; how *not* to go about capturing a Christmas goose; why you might be well advised to avoid swimming lessons; why you might like to give faith healers the widest of a wide berths; and how to deal with the neighbours from hell. But most of all learn how you can have lots of FUN whilst you're doing it all.

Just one of over many 5 star Amazon Reader's Reviews -
"It's a long time since I laughed out loud whilst reading. I started reading this book, got to the part about Marilyn Monroe and nearly wet myself laughing. Got some very strange looks from my wife and was told that my kindle would be taken from me if I didn't stop chuckling. I ended up having to put the book down because my sides were hurting so much." Geoff G.

Printed in Great Britain
by Amazon